# TEST YOURSELF!

# TEST YOURSELF!

## TEST YOUR APTITUDE, PERSONALITY AND MOTIVATION AND PLAN YOUR CAREER

### JIM BARRETT

KOGAN
PAGE

First published by Kogan Page Limited in 2000
Reprinted in 2001
Reprinted in 2003

120 Pentonville Road
London
N1 9JN
UK

22883 Quicksilver Drive
Sterling VA 20166-2012
USA

www.kogan-page.co.uk

---

British Library Cataloguing in Publication Data

A CIP record for this book is available from the British Library.

ISBN 0 7494 3320 5

---

Typeset by Jean Cussons Typesetting, Diss, Norfolk
Printed and bound in Great Britain by Biddles Ltd, *www.biddles.co.uk*

# Contents

Contents

# Introduction

## How to use this book

*Test Yourself!* provides you with comprehensive, well-proven, psychological methods that enable you to understand and make full use of your abilities.

If you follow the instructions to each chapter you will be able to build a personal profile of attributes and skills. You can use this knowledge:

- for career guidance, career planning, career development or career review;

- as a preparation for selection or assessment situations;

- for personal awareness and effectiveness;

- to gain insight into the behaviour and personality of others.

*Test Yourself!* contains three types of test:

- *Aptitudes.* These are designed to give you information about types of intelligence that are relevant to different skills and careers. Completing all of the tests will allow you to establish your likely strengths and weaknesses in order that you can: 1) know what your strengths are and find a way to use them; 2) know your weaknesses, at the same time not allowing yourself to be limited by them.

- *Personality*. These are designed to help you consider: 1) how your own style may suit some areas of work more than others, which might also suggest how you might 'grow into' or 'move on to' new, different areas of work; 2) how your understanding of behaviour helps you to work with others, who may often be very different from yourself, in order to do your best as team members.

- *Motivation*. These are designed to check out what sorts of activities appeal to you in order to relate these in a structured way to different sorts of activities. These tests should help you select work in which you are going to be interested so that you enjoy what you do.

Each of the chapters contains:

- a test, most benefit being obtained from following the rules for taking the test very carefully, especially the amount of time you should allow yourself where this is appropriate;

- instructions on how to mark the test;

- comments on what the test measures;

- advice on how to use the information from the test.

The tests can be taken in any order depending upon your interest or need.

# Testing

The use of tests is increasing. Whether you like tests or not, it is becoming difficult to avoid them. Many employers use them routinely because they find them more reliable indicators of what people can contribute than examination results, or even than someone's experience. For the individual, they can often help establish where opportunities might be available, even though an individual has no previous knowledge or experience of that area.

Here are some of the reasons you might benefit from the tests:

- to obtain some independent advice;

- to become familiar with tests in order to be less apprehensive about them in future situations where you may be 'tested' professionally;

- to gain practice in order that you ensure that you can present your qualities in the best possible light;

- to have a means of comparing your own talents in order to see where you might obtain the most satisfaction in the long term;

- to compare yourself with others in order to make full use of your advantages;

- to better understand that others might have different strengths that could complement your own;

- to understand why you 'get on with' some people better than others;

- to understand why a person may become discouraged or frustrated with what they are doing or who they are working with;

- to better appreciate what examiners or possible employers may be looking for when they use tests;

- for fun.

# Your 'hidden' ability

All of us have so much ability that never gets used! In most cases, we are not aware of all we can do. If we are, we may not know how we can best apply it.

People who are happy and successful have learnt to use their ability and, probably, keep rediscovering aspects of it.

There is, of course, no obligation to use your ability. On the other hand, frustration is often an indication that we have ability that we are not using effectively.

All of us go through moments of self-doubt. Perhaps you would like to do something or even behave in a certain way, but are unsure that you could, or think that you would be foolish to try. Often, people ask, 'What might I have become if I had had different opportunities?'

The advantage of objective tests is that they may suggest areas in which you could succeed, even though you have not yet had any experience of them. Also, they may reassure you that you may have a lot more to offer than you might suppose.

If you are failing in a certain area in which the test results suggest you should be doing well, something must be going wrong. Psychologists are used to looking for reasons for misalignment between performance and a person's true ability. Here are some of the common reasons why ability is not always readily obvious:

■ The way you were taught did not suit you. A teaching method brings out the best in one person, but 'turns off' another. Similarly, pupils do better with a teacher they like.

■ Your mental, social or emotional development was not yet ready for you to do your best. In all these areas, people develop at different rates. You might have missed out because you were not ready at the time.

■ Your own attitude worked against you. For all sorts of possible reasons, you chose not to use your ability. Possibly you did not really try because 'there would be no point'.

The timed tests in this book are designed to discover your ability in an 'abstract' way. That is, the purpose is to test whether you think in a way that has some relation to what you might study as well as to the 'real world' of work.

The assumption is that, *if you have the 'abstract' ability revealed by the test, you have the potential to translate this into something that you can actually do.*

The kind of 'ability' testing is usually called 'aptitude' testing. Other books of mine use the word 'aptitude', which means just the same as 'hidden ability'. It is very likely that this book will at least confirm some of the 'ability' you thought you had. It might also suggest that you have more potential than you thought.

Whilst having everything to gain from 'testing yourself', you have nothing to lose. Tests do not prove that you cannot do something. They can only suggest that you could do something. It is then up to you to do something about it, if you want.

# Profile matching

At the end of each major section of the book, that is, following the ability, career search and personality tests, there is a list of careers. Against each career are some tentative suggestions as to how your results on the tests may align with these.

There are two ways of using these profiles: 1) working down the career list, stopping at those that appeal to you and checking out what characteristics are suggested, seeing if you have a similar or near match; 2) working down the characteristics, stopping at those occupations which have some resemblance to your own results.

Considerable caution, as well as intuition, is required to obtain the most from matching your own characteristics to the profiles. The main purpose of this exercise is to get you thinking for yourself about how you can use your potential most effectively. Different people with different characteristics may do the same job equally successfully.

These are some points to bear in mind:

- The fact that your own results do not match those suggested does not mean that the career will not suit you. The suggestions are only intended to give an indication of some of the most likely characteristics associated with that occupation. These are not the only possible ones.

- Where you do not have the characteristics suggested, but like the sound of the occupation, always ask yourself how your own characteristics might also be suitable. Where your characteristics in one area, say motivation, coincide with many possible occupations, use the ability and personality areas to narrow down the possibilities.

- Where you seem to be suited to one career because of your potential ability, say, but to another career because of some other aspect of your potential, say personality, you are the only person who can make the decision as to what will suit you best.

- Two or more ticks against an occupation does not mean that each of these areas carries equal importance. For example, a manager might be good at visual, verbal and numerical reasoning, or only one of them.

- Where an occupation appears against which there are no ticks, this does not indicate that ability is unnecessary, but rather that none of these areas stands out as likely to be more important than the others.

■ Ticks in the abilities area indicate where some potential is likely to be required. In relation to occupations that might require a degree as a starting point, ability is likely to be required at least at the level of 'good evidence'. (The 'evidence' you can obtain from the tests is explained later on.)

This book can only act as a guide and help to structure your thinking about your potential. Get further advice wherever you can, either from people who know you or from people who have expertise, such as careers counsellors.

# How to do the tests

## The aptitude tests

The timed aptitude tests have 'right or wrong' answers. To establish whether there is evidence that you have potential in these areas, they need to be taken in accordance with the instructions provided.

The aim of these particular tests is to make you think about what sorts of problem solving are easier for you and what might be more difficult. This then leads on to a consideration of whether the tests' results can suggest that you would find one area of study or a particular career easier to accomplish than another. Of course, you are not obliged to do what is easiest, and evidence from some of the other tests that look at career preferences might suggest that you are very motivated to achieve at something that you might find comparatively difficult. In the end, is it up to you to decide what will make you feel successful.

You can do the aptitude tests in any order you like. It is not necessary to do all of them, but most benefit is obtained if you do, since you then gain an aptitude 'profile', which shows your strong and weaker areas clearly. This is useful when thinking about applying yourself to work, because most jobs require different abilities in different measures.

Do not get discouraged if you find the tests difficult. They are designed to be so! The intention is to really stretch your mind.

There are more test items than you will be able to do in the time allowed, so the fact that you do not get to the end of the tests does not mean you are not doing well. If you try your best on all the tests, the profile that is produced can give you very useful information about your talents.

## Instructions for taking the timed aptitude tests

It is helpful if you test yourself in the strict way that you might experience in other test situations. This will prepare you in the best way for being tested formally for college examinations or for assessments when you seek employment. The following advice and instructions are similar to what you will be told on such occasions:

1. When taking the tests, ensure that you have a place where you can work quietly without interruption. You will need an accurate watch. One that 'counts down' is preferred. Also make sure that the light is good and that you have pencils and rough paper to work on.

2. Read the instructions carefully and do not start until you are clear about what you have to do. This is most important, as you will waste time if you have to turn back to read the instructions once you have already started.

3. You have to do as many items as you can in the time allowed. Do not try to rush through to get everything done. If you do so, you are likely to make mistakes, because the

tests have been designed to be almost impossible to finish within the short time given.

4. Work as quickly and as carefully as you can. Try not to guess. On some tests guessing will count against you, so try hard to get the correct answer. (Guessing counts against you in many of the tests you are likely to take during your education and your career.)

5. When you are absolutely sure you are ready, turn over the page and start your time. Stop exactly at the end of the time allowed.

## Marking and interpreting your aptitude test results

After you have completed the test, you can check your answers to see how many were correct. Then you can see how well you did by referring to the chart.

Your score will fall into one of four grades, comparing you with other males and females who also took the tests:

av - average aptitude compared with most people
aa - above average aptitude, possibly degree level potential
waa - well above aptitude, at least degree level potential
ea - exceptional aptitude

As you will be comparing yourself with a broad group of people, it is possible you may be comparing yourself unfairly. This could be, for example, because you are younger or older than this broad group who are, on average, about 28 years old. Therefore you might be quicker on some tests, but slower on others, than this group. Some allowance for age is made, as you will see when you come to score the tests. Another example is that of gender, since, on average, females tend to do better than males on verbal tests, whilst males often do better on some spatial tests. However, there are so many different factors and circumstances to be taken into account that you will have to be your own judge as to whether you might be at a disadvantage on any of the tests, allowing yourself some extra marks to compensate if you think that is fair.

## How to do the personality and motivation tests

These do not have 'right or wrong' answers to the questions. It is your opinion that counts. You can approach these tests in your own way and take as long as you like.

# Other books of mine

*Career, Aptitude & Selection Tests* is a companion volume to *Test Yourself!*, and uses similar, structured measures to discover potential that can be useful in planning and developing your career.

*Total Leadership* is about gaining awareness of how to inspire and motivate people with whom you come into contact.

# Part 1

# Aptitudes

# Chapter 1
# Visual reasoning test

There are two types of problem in this test. In one type, you have to decide which of the objects you are shown is the 'odd one out'. This will be the one that in some way makes it different from the others in the set.

In the second type of problem you are shown a sequence of objects or shapes. Your task is to choose, from the alternatives you are given, the one that would come next in line where there is a large question mark. The examples will show you how to do this test.

## Example 1

**Which is the odd one out?**

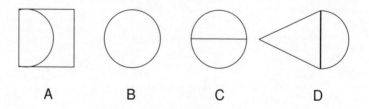

|  A  |  B  |  C  |  D  |

## Example 2

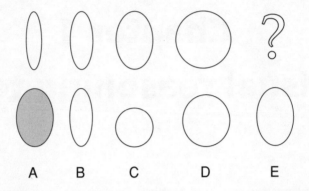

In Example 1, B is the correct answer. It is the only curved shape that does not also have a straight line.

In Example 2, the figures are of a circle that is turning. The figures can also be seen as a shape that is expanding by equal amounts until it becomes a full circle. The next step would be for the circle to turn by the same amount as before, or to decrease by the same amount as before. E is the correct answer. Although A is the correct shape, there is no reason why it should be shaded. D is not quite the correct size because it has not turned enough. B is not correct because it has turned too much. C is the wrong size and has not turned at all.

You have 10 minutes to do as many as you can. Begin as soon as you are ready.

1.                    Which is the odd one out?

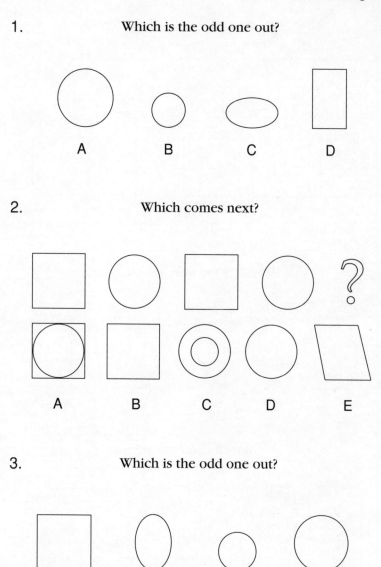

2.                    Which comes next?

3.                    Which is the odd one out?

4. Which comes next?

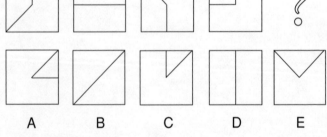

5. Which is the odd one out?

6. Which comes next?

7.                    Which is the odd one out?

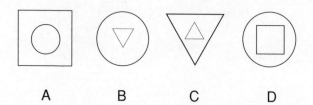

A          B          C          D

8.                    Which comes next?

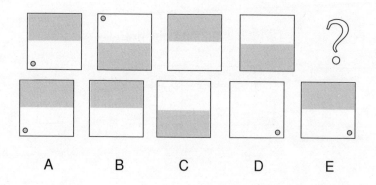

A          B          C          D          E

9.                    Which is the odd one out?

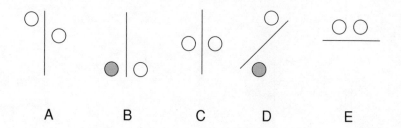

A          B          C          D          E

10. Which comes next?

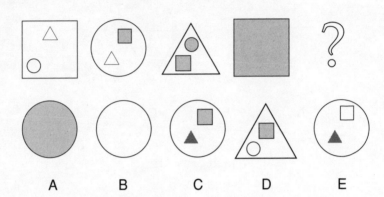

| A | B | C | D | E |

11. Which is the odd one out?

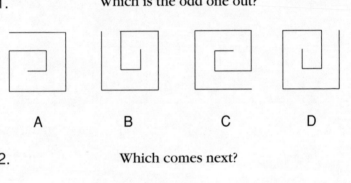

| A | B | C | D |

12. Which comes next?

| A | B | C | D | E |

13. Which is the odd one out?

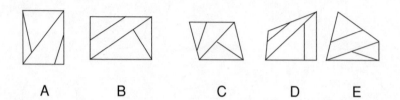

A      B      C      D      E

14. Which comes next?

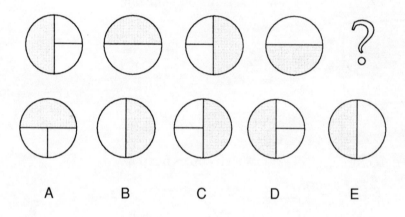

A      B      C      D      E

15. Which is the odd one out?

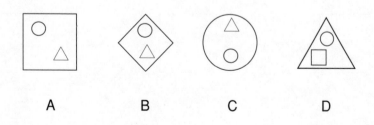

A      B      C      D

16. Which comes next?

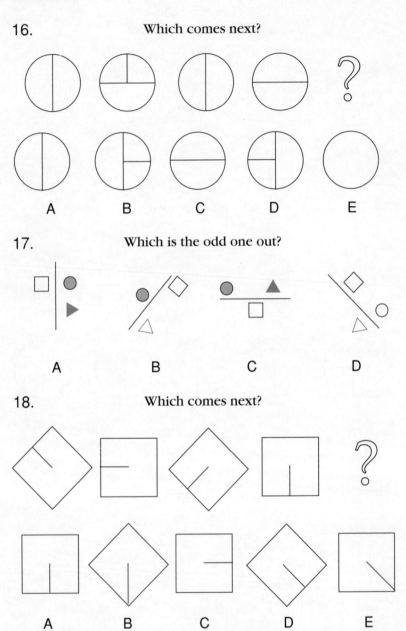

17. Which is the odd one out?

18. Which comes next?

19.          Which is the odd one out?

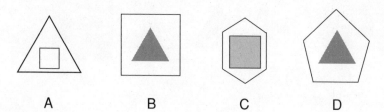

   A          B          C          D

20.          Which comes next?

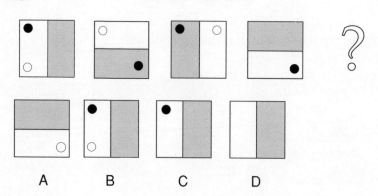

   A       B       C       D

21.          Which is the odd one out?

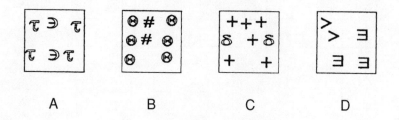

   A          B          C          D

22. Which comes next?

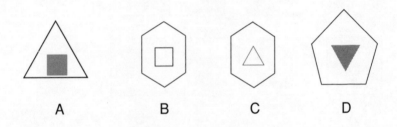

A          B          C          D

23. Which is the odd one out?

A          B          C          D

24. Which comes next?

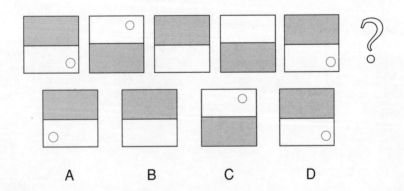

A          B          C          D

25.

Which is the odd one out?

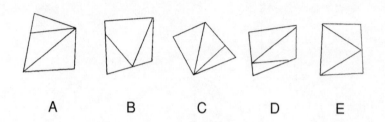

A          B          C          D          E

26.          Which comes next?

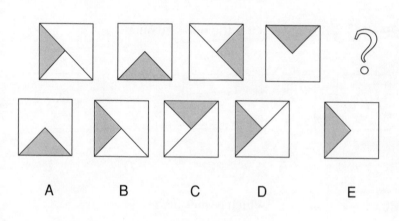

A          B          C          D          E

27.          Which is the odd one out?

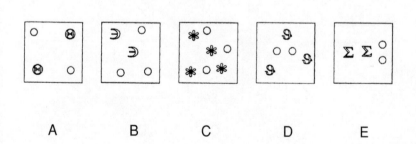

A          B          C          D          E

28. Which comes next?

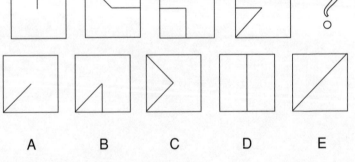

A     B     C     D

29. Which is the odd one out?

A     B     C     D     E

30. Which comes next?

A     B     C     D     E

31.          Which is the odd one out?

      A          B          C          D          E

32.          Which is the odd one out?

      A          B          C          D          E

# Answers to visual reasoning test

| | | | |
|---|---|---|---|
| 1 – d | 9 – e | 17 – d | 25 – e |
| 2 – b | 10 – a | 18 – d | 26 – b |
| 3 – a | 11 – b | 19 – a | 27 – b |
| 4 – e | 12 – a | 20 – b | 28 – b |
| 5 – c | 13 – d | 21 – d | 29 – c |
| 6 – a | 14 – d | 22 – a | 30 – d |
| 7 – c | 15 – c | 23 – a | 31 – b |
| 8 – a | 16 – a | 24 – b | 32 – d |

## Obtaining the total score

| | | |
|---|---|---|
| | number correct = | _____ |
| | plus 3 if no mistakes | +3 _____ |
| | Total score = | _____ |

## Establishing level of potential

| average | above average | well above average | exceptional |
|---|---|---|---|
| 1–6 | 7–13 | 14–20 | 21+ |

## Interpretation

This is one of the tests that is closest to measuring 'natural' intelligence, that is, intelligence that you are born with, rather than abilities you acquired. Although the verbal and numerical tests are also reasoning tests, the ability to read and to work with numbers has had to be learnt. Therefore the visual test is one of the 'purer' measures of aptitude, testing your reasoning with clues that do not have words or numbers. However, it is not the 'best' measure of innate intelligence, since some highly intelligent people do not do well on this test – they may require words or numbers to express their intelligence.

If you do better on the visual test than on the verbal or numerical reasoning tests, it often follows that you have a leaning towards science. When aptitude on the visual test is not accompanied by success on the numerical test as well, the leaning is towards those sciences that are less obviously numerical, such as the biological sciences. When numerical reasoning is also strong, the leaning tends more towards the physical and chemical sciences, as well as technology and engineering. When verbal reasoning accompanies strong *visual* reasoning, the preference is often to move more towards the social sciences.

People who do well on the visual test are often good at detail and at researching information, whether it is in science or in areas such as historical research.

# Chapter 2
# Numerical reasoning test

In this test you are given numbers that connect in some way. They connect along the row, but there is also a relationship with the numbers that are above or below each other. Sometimes a number is missing and a space mark, or line, ( - ), has been put in its place. One of the numbers has been replaced by a question mark ( ? ).

From the information given, you have to find the number that would replace the question mark.

## Example

| 1 | – | 3 | ? | |
|---|---|---|---|---|
| – | 4 | 6 | 8 | Answer = |

*The most logical answer is 4; it fits the sequence 1, 2, 3, 4 because a 2 could replace the space mark. Also, 4 is half of 8, in the same way that 3 is half of 6, 2 is half of 4, and 1 is half of 2. The answer, 4, makes all the numbers fit together logically.*

| 1 | 2 | 3 | 4 | |
|---|---|---|---|---|
| 2 | 4 | 6 | 8 | Answer = 4 |

# Example

| 1 | – | 9 | ? |
|---|---|---|---|
| 2 | 6 | – | 54 | Answer =

*The numbers in the lower line are always twice the number in the line above. Also, from left to right, each number is multiplied three times.*

| 1 | 3 | 9 | 27 |
|---|---|---|---|
| 2 | 6 | 18 | 54 | Answer = 27

Working out the correct numbers for the empty spaces can help you find the number that can replace the question mark. You have eight minutes to do as many as you can. It is important to work as quickly as possible in order to get as many right as possible in the time allowed.

Begin as soon as you are ready.

1.
| 4 | 3 | 2 | ? |
|---|---|---|---|
| 4 | – | 2 | 1 | Answer =

2.
| 2 | 4 | 6 | – |
|---|---|---|---|
| 4 | ? | 12 | 16 | Answer =

3.
| 1 | ? | 5 | 7 | – |
|---|---|---|---|---|
| – | 6 | – | – | 18 | Answer =

4.
| – | – | 8 | 4 | ? |
|---|---|---|---|---|
| 64 | 32 | – | – | 4 | Answer =

**Test Yourself!**

| 5. | 2 | 3 | ? | – | 12 | |
| | – | – | 5 | 8 | 12 | Answer = |

| 6. | 3 | 6 | 9 | 12 | |
| | 9 | ? | – | 36 | Answer = |

| 7. | 25 | 16 | 9 | 4 | |
| | – | 4 | ? | 2 | Answer = |

| 8. | 3 | 7 | ? | – | |
| | 4 | 8 | 16 | 32 | Answer = |

| 9. | 7 | 12 | 22 | – | 82 | |
| | 4 | 9 | 19 | ? | | Answer = |

| 10. | 13 | 14 | 16 | ? | 28 | |
| | 1 | – | 4 | – | 8 | Answer = |

| 11. | 3 | 7 | 16 | 35 | ? | |
| | 1 | 2 | 3 | – | 5 | Answer = |

| 12. | 11 | 14 | – | ? | |
| | 33 | 42 | 60 | 87 | Answer = |

| 13. | 3 | 6 | 5 | 8 | 7 | – | |
| | 7 | 11 | 11 | 15 | 15 | ? | Answer = |

14.
| ? | 5 | 7 | 12 | – | |
|---|---|---|----|----|---|
| 3 | – | 8 | 13 | 21 | Answer = |


15.
| 4 | 5 | 8 | 10 | ? | 20 | |
|----|---|----|----|----|----|---|
| 10 | 8 | 20 | 16 | 40 | – | Answer = |


16.
| 3 | 7 | 5 | ? | 7 | 11 | |
|---|---|---|---|---|----|---|
| – | 4 | 2 | 4 | 2 | – | Answer = |


17.
| 5 | 10 | 7 | 12 | – | |
|----|----|----|----|----|---|
| 10 | 30 | ? | 60 | 54 | Answer = |


18.
| 6 | 13 | 20 | – | 34 | |
|---|----|----|---|----|---|
| ? | 24 | 37 | – | 63 | Answer = |


19.
| 0 | 5 | 3 | 13 | 11 | ? | |
|---|---|----|----|----|---|---|
| 5 | – | 10 | 2 | 20 | – | Answer = |


20.
| 13 | ? | 22 | 31 | 53 | |
|----|----|----|----|----|---|
| 78 | 45 | – | 93 | – | Answer = |

# Answers to numerical reasoning test

| 1 – 1 | 6 – 18 | 11 – 74 | 16 – 9 |
|-------|--------|---------|--------|
| 2 – 8 | 7 – 2 | 12 – 29 | 17 – 28 |
| 3 – 3 | 8 – 15 | 13 – 21 | 18 – 11 |
| 4 – 2 | 9 – 39 | 14 – 2 | 19 – 31 |
| 5 – 5 | 10 – 20 | 15 – 16 | 20 – 9 |

## Obtaining the total score

| | number correct = | _____ | |
|---|---|---|---|
| | plus 2 if no mistakes | +2 _____ | |
| | Total score = | _____ | |

## Establishing level of potential

| average | above average | well above average | exceptional |
|---------|---------------|--------------------|-------------|
| 1-4 | 5-7 | 8-12 | 13+ |

## Interpretation

The numerical test is much more than a test of arithmetic, since it involves working out the relationship between numbers and detecting a pattern. Although some arithmetical skills are required, the test measures mathematical potential in a broader way than the skill of arithmetic does. Often people who do well on this test say that they have never done particularly well with mathematics, whereas it is only lack of practice involving the 'rules of numbers' – how to subtract, divide, and so on – that has made mathematics difficult for them.

Potential in this area could point to many careers where the analysis of quantitative data is important. Such areas might be as diverse as marketing and science, because both involve the use of statistics. If you have a high score, you would probably readily grasp financial information in business, even though you may be somewhat slow or careless with accounting.

If your score is much higher than those for visual and verbal reasoning, you will probably prefer a career that specifically uses this potential in the first instance. You would probably prefer to follow courses that have a mathematical element, depending upon your motivation. If your interests are commercial, then economics or business studies might suit you. If your interests are more technical, then courses in science, engineering or computing might suit you.

If your score is accompanied by high verbal reasoning, then you might prefer a career where you can use numerical as well as verbal ability, so commerce, business or teaching would be some of the possibilities for you to consider. When your numerical score is accompanied by visual reasoning potential, your leaning is likely to be more scientific or technical, at least at the outset of your career, though your eventual direction will be influenced by your personality.

# Chapter 3
# Verbal analysis test

In this test we are looking at the way you can draw logical conclusions from the information you have been given. There is always sufficient information for you to work out the correct answer. You should not draw upon any previous experience or information you suppose might be relevant. You are given some facts and some possible answers. Tick the letter that corresponds to the correct answer.

## Example 1

The town of Newport is further west than the town of Flatpeak, although not so far west as the town of Daybridge.

Which town is furthest east?
Answers:     a) Newport   b) Daybridge   c) Flatpeak

The answer cannot be a) because Newport is west of Flatpeak. It cannot be b) because Daybridge is even further west, so Flatpeak must be to the east of both other towns. The answer is c).

## Example 2

Fred, Mack and John all have two different cars each. One of them does not have a Ford. Mack is the only one to have a Ferrari. John has a Ford. Fred and Mack have Buicks.

Who has a Rolls-Royce?
a) Fred        b) Mack        c) John

The answer is c). It cannot be a), because Fred has a Ford and a Buick. It cannot be b), because Mack has a Ferrari and a Buick.

Because of the amount of information you are sometimes asked to deal with, it is recommended that you have a piece of scrap paper so that you can, if you wish, draw and make notes or plans. Diagrams, like the following, are often helpful:

|  | **PEOPLE:** | | |
| --- | --- | --- | --- |
| **CARS:** | Fred | Mack | John |
| Ferrari | ✗ | ✔ | ✗ |
| Buick | ✔ | ✔ | ✗ |
| Ford | ✔ | ✗ | ✔ |
| Rolls-Royce | | | |

You have ten minutes to do as much of the test as you can. Get your scrap paper and pencil ready in case you need it. Work as accurately and as fast as you can. When you are ready, start the clock and begin.

1. Emma lives further up the hill than Jane. Pauline lives further up the hill than Emma.

   Who lives furthest up the hill?
   a) Emma        b) Jane        c) Pauline

2. All the girls like sports. Sue and Josie like tennis, while Sally and Anne like running. Both Sue and Anne like swimming.

Who likes tennis and swimming?
a) Sue   b) Josie   c) Sally   d) Anne

3. Who likes swimming and running?
a) Sue   b) Josie   c) Sally   d) Anne

4. Mr Everton and Mr Soames have longer holidays that Mr Francke. Mr Porter has a shorter holiday than Mr Francke, while Mr Peters has a longer holiday than Mr Francke.

Who has the shortest holiday?
a) Mr Everton      b) Mr Soames      c) Mr Francke
d) Mr Porter       e) Mr Peters

5. Toby, Rob and Frank all take a holiday by the sea, while Sam, Jo and Tony go hiking in the mountains. Frank, Sam and Jo travel by air. Jo, Rob and Tony do not enjoy their holiday.

Who goes to the sea and does not enjoy their holiday?
a) Toby   b) Rob   c) Frank   d) Sam   e) Jo   f) Tony

6. Who does not travel by air and goes hiking?
a) Toby   b) Rob   c) Frank   d) Sam   e) Jo   f) Tony

7. In reverse order, the most popular holiday tours offered by a travel company are Toronto, Florida, Rome and Paris, although Rome is extremely popular whatever the time of year. After a marketing promotion, Toronto becomes more popular than Rome, but less popular than Florida.

Which tour is most popular after the marketing promotion?

a) Toronto   b) Florida   c) Rome   d) Paris

8. Which tour is least popular after the marketing promotion?

a) Toronto   b) Florida   c) Rome   d) Paris

9. Fred, John, Garth and Joe all have children. Fred and John are the only two to have boys. John and Joe take their children to school by bus, while it is short enough to school for the others to walk. To be fair, Fred and Joe are car owners, and sometimes do use their cars to get the children to school.

Who owns a car, but usually goes to work by bus?

a) Fred       b) Joe       c) John       d) Garth

10. Who does not own a car and has a daughter?

a) Fred       b) Joe       c) John       d) Garth

11. In a museum, Modern Sculpture is to be found on the floor below Watercolours. Greek Pottery is on the floor above the Oil Paintings. The top floor contains the Italian Collection. Watercolours are on the same floor as South American Art, whereas the Oil Paintings are on the floor below Modern Sculpture.

What is to be found on the lowest floor?

a) Modern Sculpture     b) Watercolours
c) Greek Pottery        d) Oil Paintings
e) Italian Collection   f) South American Art

12.  Which two are on the same floor?
     a)  Modern Sculpture and Greek Pottery
     b)  Watercolours and Oil Paintings
     c)  Oil Paintings and South American Art
     d)  None of these

13.  Casey, Stuart, Ritchie, Billie and Colin all buy their own
     vehicles. Casey and Colin have room for three passengers
     as well as themselves. The others have room for only one
     passenger besides themselves. Ritchie and Casey have
     good front tyres, though the other tyres on all of the
     other vehicles are dangerous. Casey and Billie have vehi-
     cles that take diesel fuel. The others have vehicles that
     take petrol.

     Who can take three passengers in their diesel vehicle?
     a) Casey   b) Stuart   c) Ritchie   d) Billie   e) Colin

14.  How many people have dangerous tyres on diesel
     vehicles that have room for only one passenger?
     a) 5     b) 4     c) 3     d) 2     e) 1     f) None

15.  Who can take only one passenger, but has some good
     tyres?
     a)  Casey        b)  Stuart        c)  Ritchie
     d)  Billie       e)  Colin

16.  Mrs Booth has difficulty feeding her four children as each
     one will eat only certain foods. Sharon and Robina will
     eat rice and lamb. Kelly and Sharon are the only ones
     who like bread and cheese. Kelly and Sam both eat
     chicken and bread.

Which is the only food that Sharon does not eat?
a) bread     b) chicken     c) lamb
d) rice      e) cheese

17. Who eats cheese, chicken and bread?
    a) Sharon     b) Kelly     c) Robina
    d) Sam

18. Who does not eat cheese, but does eat lamb and rice?
    a) Sharon     b) Kelly     c) Robina
    d) Sam

19. Which food will be acceptable to most of the children?
    a) bread     b) rice     c) lamb
    d) cheese    e) chicken

20. Mr Marx's and Mr Bagshaw's cars are black. The others
    have red ones. Mr Bagshaw and Mrs Chance have a white
    stripe on the sides of their cars. Miss Jenkins has a blue
    stripe on the side of her car. Mr Fleming and Mr Marx
    have silver stripes on the sides of their cars. Miss Jenkins'
    and Mr Fleming's have blue upholstery, while the others
    have white.

    Who has a car with blue upholstery and a silver stripe?
    a) Mr Bagshaw     b) Miss Jenkins     c) Mrs Chance
    d) Mr Fleming     e) Mr Marx

21. Who has a car with a silver stripe and white upholstery?
    a) Mr Bagshaw     b) Miss Jenkins     c) Mrs Chance
    d) Mr Fleming     e) Mr Marx

22. Who has the red car with a blue stripe and matching upholstery?
    a) Mr Bagshaw    b) Miss Jenkins    c) Mrs Chance
    d) Mr Fleming    e) Mr Marx

23. In a 'knockout' basketball competition, Centurions are beaten by Raiders. Saracens beat Centurions. Saracens are beaten by Raiders and Aztecs. Centurions and Raiders are beaten by Aztecs.

    How many games do Saracens win?
    a) 1    b) 2    c) 3    d) 4    e) 0

24. How many games do Raiders win?
    a) 1    b) 2    c) 3    d) 4    e) 0

25. Who emerges as the champions?
    a) Raiders    b) Saracens    c) Aztecs
    d) Centurions

26. Stopping at the shop, on the way to school, Cheryl and Tom are the only ones not to buy chocolate. Of the five children, four of them, including Laura, buy fudge. Unlike the others, Sally, Cheryl and Sandy do not buy any toffee. In fact, Cheryl only buys fruit gums as she does not like other kinds of sweets.

    Who only had a piece of toffee and a piece of fudge?
    a) Sally    b) Cheryl    c) Laura
    d) Tom    e) Sandy

27. Who had three sweets?
    a) Sally    b) Cheryl    c) Laura
    d) Tom    e) Sandy

28. Who are the two people who took the same number and type of sweets?
    a) Sally and Laura
    b) Sally and Tom
    c) Laura and Tom
    d) Tom and Sandy
    e) Sandy and Sally

29. In total, how many sweets were taken by the group?
    a) 7   b) 8   c) 9   d) 10   e) 11   f) 12

30. Jane, Rachel and Tessa are girls who are wearing a jacket, coat or skirt in blue, green or red. None of these articles of clothing are in the same colour and each girl is wearing something of each colour. The coat belonging to Tessa is not green. Rachel's jacket and Jane's skirt are the same colour. Tessa's skirt is red. Her jacket, Rachel's skirt and Jane's coat are all the same colour.

    What colour is Tessa's coat?
    a) blue   b) green   c) red

31. What colour is Jane's jacket?
    a) blue   b) green   c) red

32. Which girl has the green coat?
    a) Jane   b) Rachel   c) Tessa

33. Which girl has the blue jacket?
    a) Jane   b) Rachel   c) Tessa

# Answers to verbal analysis test

| | | | |
|---|---|---|---|
| 1 – c | 10 – d | 18 – c | 26 – d |
| 2 – a | 11 – d | 19 – a | 27 – c |
| 3 – d | 12 – a | 20 – d | 28 – e |
| 4 – d | 13 – a | 21 – e | 29 – d |
| 5 – b | 14 – e | 22 – b | 30 – a |
| 6 – f | 15 – c | 23 – a | 31 – c |
| 7 – d | 16 – b | 24 – b | 32 – a |
| 8 – b | 17 – b | 25 – c | 33 – b |
| 9 – b | | | |

## Obtaining the total score

| | | | |
|---|---|---|---|
| | number correct = | _____ | |
| | plus 3 if no mistakes | +3 _____ | |
| | Total score = | _____ | |

## Establishing level of potential

| average | above average | well above average | exceptional |
|---|---|---|---|
| 1–7 | 8–11 | 12–15 | 16+ |

## Interpretation

A similar test, with different items, was also given in my book *Career, Aptitude & Selection Tests*, where it was called 'Critical dissection'. This is exactly the skill it demands, almost as though you have to be a detective, weighing up clues and deriving some logical conclusion from what often appears to be confused. It requires a critical analysis of the facts given, but it also demands that you make logical assumptions about information that can only be derived from what you have been given so far, since vital information is not given to you directly. In this test you need the ability to be able to 'put two and two together'.

In the same way as the other reasoning tests, the verbal test requires you to analyse the situation with which you are presented. The verbal test assesses whether you can reason using words, as opposed to numbers or visual information. If you do better on this test than the other reasoning tests, you will almost inevitably be drawn towards careers where you are involved with communications in some form. High verbal as well as numerical reasoning or visual reasoning is frequently a good indicator of 'academic' potential across the humanities, social sciences and biological sciences.

Obviously, the verbal reasoning test requires some amount of vocabulary, but the complexity of the words themselves is not what is being measured. Often, people whose second language is English do well on this test because they have the logical mind to enable them to achieve with it, even though their level of vocabulary is much lower. It is worth comparing your own score on the verbal reasoning test with the vocabulary test. If you obtain high scores on both, it really does seem that a career involving words and communications would suit you. If you are high on verbal reasoning, but low on vocabulary, you will probably use your ability in talking with people, perhaps in management or in some other form of direct, person to person, communications. If your vocabulary is higher, you will probably do well in some written or more formal communications.

# Chapter 4
# Sequential reasoning test

You are given a string of shapes. You have to work out which two shapes are missing from the string. The missing shapes have been replaced with a 1 and a 2. Choose the correct answers from the possible answers provided on the page. Write in the correct letter that goes with the missing shape. There is space to write in your answers on the right of the page.

Possible answers:

A    B    C    D    E    F    G

**Example 1**

## Example 2

Answers

$1 = A$

$2 = F$

In Example 1, there is a sequence of alternate squares and circles. The fourth in the sequence is a missing circle, so F is correct from the possible answers. Number 13 in the sequence, where a 2 has been placed, should have a square, so D has been written in as the correct answer.

In Example 2, the sequence is triangle, circle, square. A small, white circle would go where the 1 has been placed, so A has been written in. In the sequence, the circles are alternately small and large. A large circle would go where the 2 has been placed, so F has been written in.

The real test is done in just this way. Find the correct answer from those given on each page and write in the letter in the space provided for answers. Both parts must be correct to score.

You have 15 minutes to do as many as you can.

A    B    C    D    E    F

1.

  1   2   3   4   5   6   7   8

☐ ○ 1 ○ ☐ ○ ☐ 2

☐ ○ ☐ ○ ☐ ○ ☐

  9   10   11   12   13   14   15

1 =
2 =

2.

◁ ○ ☐ ◁ ○ ☐ ◁ ○

1 ◁ ○ ☐ ◁ 2 ☐

1 =
2 =

3.

☐ ○ ☐ ☐ ○ ☐ ☐ 1

☐ ☐ ○ ☐ ☐ ○ 2 ☐

1 =
2 =

4.

☐ ○ ■ ☐ ○ ■ 1 ○

■ ☐ ○ 2 ☐ ○ ■

1 =
2 =

47

**Test Yourself!**

A    B    C    D    E    F

5.

◁ ○ □ ◁ ○ □ 1      1 =

□ ◁ ○ □ ◁ ○ 2      2 =

6.

□ ○ ■ 1 ○ ■ □ ○      1 =

■ □ ○ 2 □ ○ ■      2 =

7.

□ ○ □ □ ○ □ 1 ○      1 =

□ 2 ○ □ □ ○ □      2 =

8.

1 ○ ■ ○ ○ ■ ○ ○      1 =

■ 2 ○ ■ ○      2 =

A  B  C  D  E  F  G  H  I

9.

$1 =$

$2 =$

10.

$1 =$

$2 =$

11.

$1 =$

$2 =$

12.

$1 =$

$2 =$

A    B    C    D    E    F    G    H    I    J    K    L

13.

■ 1 □ ■ ■ □ □ 2⌐
⌐ ■ □ □ ■

1 =
2 =

14.

△ ○ ■ 1 △ ○ ■ ⌐
⌐ ■ 2 ○ ■

1 =
2 =

15.

△ ■ 1 ○ 2 ■ ● ⌐
⌐ ○ △ ■ ● ○ △

1 =
2 =

16.

1 ■ ○ △ ○ 2 ○ ⌐
⌐ △ ○ ■ ○ △ ○ □

1 =
2 =

50

A   B   C   D   E   F   G   H   I   J   K   L

17.

1 =
2 =

18.

1 =
2 =

19.

1 =
2 =

20.

1 =
2 =

**Test Yourself!**

A B C D E F G H I J K L M N O P Q R

21.

△ ○ 1 ■ △ ○ □ □ ⌐  1 =

◺ ▲ 2 □ □ △  2 =

22.

1 △ ▤ ○ △ △ ■ ○ ⌐  1 =

◺ △ △ ■ 2 △  2 =

23.

▲ □ ○ △ 1 □ ○ ⌐  1 =

◺ △ ▲ □ ○ 2 ▲ □  2 =

24.

○ ⊕ ■ ▲ ○ ○ ⊞ ▲ ⌐  1 =

◺ ● 1 □ 2 ● ● □ △  2 =

52

A B C D E F G H I J K L M N O P Q R

**25.**

1 =
2 =

**26.**

1 =
2 =

**27.**

1 =
2 =

**28.**

1 =
2 =

△ ■ ○ ● △ □ ○ □ ■ ● ▲ ▲ ⊕ △ △ ⊞ ⊕ ⊞

A  B C D E F G  H I J K  L M  N O P  Q  R

29.

■ △ ○ ○ ▲ □ ▲ 1 ⟩   1 =

○ △ ⊞ △ 2 ○ △    2 =

30.

△ 1 ■ ○ ⊕ △ ■ ■ ⟩   1 =

○ ⊕ △ ■ ■ ○ 2    2 =

31.

1 ● □ ○ ⊞ △ ○ □ ● ⟩   1 =

□ △ ⊕ 2 ○ □ ▲ ○    2 =

32.

1 △ ● ⊕ ■ △ ● ⟩   1 =

⊕ ■ △ ● ⊕ 2    2 =

# Answers to sequential reasoning test

| | | | | | | | |
|---|---|---|---|---|---|---|---|
| 1 1=E 2=D | 9 1=B 2=G | 17 1=B 2=J | 25 1=F 2=M |
| 2 1=C 2=D | 10 1=F 2=G | 18 1=G 2=A | 26 1=I 2=B |
| 3 1=A 2=C | 11 1=B 2=D | 19 1=F 2=B | 27 1=E 2=H |
| 4 1=C 2=F | 12 1=A 2=I | 20 1=G 2=G | 28 1=F 2=J |
| 5 1=D 2=E | 13 1=H 2=I | 21 1=H 2=C | 29 1=C 2=J |
| 6 1=E 2=F | 14 1=I 2=A | 22 1=E 2=C | 30 1=B 2=M |
| 7 1=C 2=E | 15 1=D 2=E | 23 1=K 2=A | 31 1=E 2=F |
| 8 1=A 2=A | 16 1=G 2=H | 24 1=G 2=O | 32 1=I 2=I |

## Obtaining the total score

| | | | |
|---|---|---|---|
| | number correct = | _____ | |
| | plus 3 if no mistakes | +3 _____ | |
| | Total score = | _____ | |

## Establishing level of potential

| average | above average | well above average | exceptional |
|---|---|---|---|
| 1–8 | 9–12 | 13–18 | 19+ |

## Interpretation

In this test a number of sequences thread through each other. It is a complex matter to be able to detect each thread and see how they overlap in order to detect the missing components. In the sense that it contains only visual information, the sequential reasoning test seems to be similar to the perceptual test. However, the way of reasoning in this test is qualitatively different.

The purpose the sequential reasoning test serves as a further check on your underlying potential. Although most people find this test very demanding indeed, if not downright difficult, it can often show potential that does not appear on the visual, numerical or verbal reasoning tests. In other words, if you obtain a higher score on the sequential reasoning test than on the other reasoning tests, you can be sure that you have potential that you have not used so far.

Often, people with this type of result turn out to be much more successful in their careers than their merely academic results might have predicted. If your score is well above average, compared with your other reasoning scores, you will probably find yourself eventually in a career where you work at the same level or above the level of many graduates or professional people, even though you have no qualifications to speak of yourself. You will probably 'work your way up' in your career, getting promoted because you prove you have initiative and capability, rather than because you have passed examinations that have tested formal skills. You can think quickly and are probably most effective in dealing with practical situations involving people.

Where potential seen on the sequential reasoning test is accompanied by high scores on the other reasoning tests, this would indicate strong and broad abilities that would probably be expressed in high attainments at school and college, and success in a career involving management.

# Chapter 5
# Spatial recognition test

This test explores how easily you can 'see' and turn around objects in space.

You will be shown a shape in the middle of the page. Below it are five other shapes. Each of these is numbered. You have to decide whether each of the alternatives is *identical* to the original shape. A shape will be the same as the original if it has been turned over or around. It will not be the same as the original if the proportions or parts have been changed. You are to answer each question with a 'Y' for Yes and 'N' for No.

Remember, shapes that are identical to the original, but have been turned around or have been turned over, are marked 'Y'. If it is not the same or a 'mirror image' you mark 'N'. Try to 'see' the result in your mind.

**Test Yourself!**

## Example

(Answers to example items: 1 N  2 N  3 Y  4 Y  5 N)

You have to work as quickly and as accurately as you can. You have 10 minutes. Start as soon as you are ready.

58

1

2

3

4

5

6

7

8

9

10

11

12

13

14

15

16

17

18

19

20

21 22 23

24 25

26          27          28

29          30

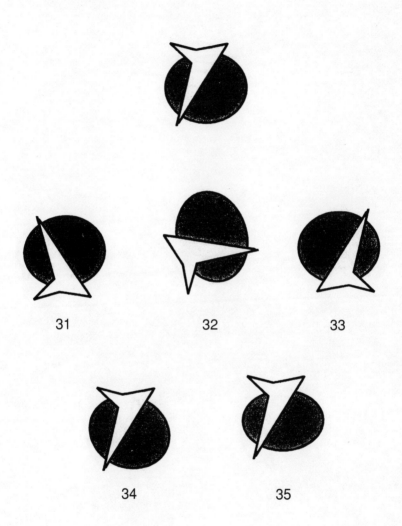

31          32          33

34          35

36          37          38

39          40

41          42          43

44          45

46

47

48

49

50

51  52  53

54  55

56

57

58

59

60

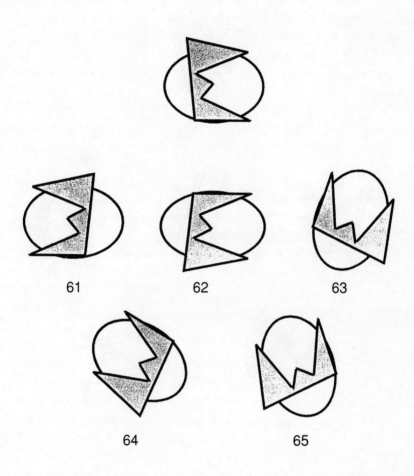

61          62          63

64          65

66          67          68

69          70

## Answers to spatial recognition test

| | | | | |
|---|---|---|---|---|
| 1 - N | 15 - N | 29 - N | 43 - Y | 57 - Y |
| 2 - N | 16 - N | 30 - Y | 44 - Y | 58 - Y |
| 3 - Y | 17 - Y | 31 - N | 45 - N | 59 - N |
| 4 - Y | 18 - Y | 32 - N | 46 - N | 60 - N |
| 5 - Y | 19 - Y | 33 - Y | 47 - Y | 61 - N |
| 6 - Y | 20 - Y | 34 - N | 48 - N | 62 - N |
| 7 - N | 21 - Y | 35 - N | 49 - Y | 63 - Y |
| 8 - N | 22 - Y | 36 - Y | 50 - N | 64 - Y |
| 9 - Y | 23 - N | 37 - N | 51 - N | 65 - Y |
| 10 - N | 24 - N | 38 - N | 52 - N | 66 - Y |
| 11 - Y | 25 - Y | 39 - Y | 53 - N | 67 - N |
| 12 - N | 26 - N | 40 - Y | 54 - N | 68 - Y |
| 13 - N | 27 - Y | 41 - N | 55 - Y | 69 - Y |
| 14 - Y | 28 - N | 42 - N | 56 - N | 70 - N |

## Obtaining the total score

| | | | |
|---|---|---|---|
| | number correct = | _____ | |
| | take away half the number of errors | - _____ | |
| | Total score = | _____ | |

## Establishing level of potential

| average | above average | well above average | exceptional |
|---|---|---|---|
| 1–26 | 27–34 | 35–42 | 43+ |

## Interpretation

A similar test, with different items, was also given in my book *Career, Aptitude & Selection Tests*. It is a useful test because it often detects raw, natural potential to perceive abstract problems as well as those that often relate to art and design.

The ability to cope with rotating shapes is in some way the equivalent of 'turning things over in the mind' – an ability that is relevant to many areas of endeavour where flexibility of thinking is important. Often, people who do well on this test are seen as original or imaginative because they seem to create new possibilities or outcomes. If you can do well on this test you may well be perceived as someone who comes up with ideas that are new or different

How this potential expresses itself is usually determined by how it combines with other areas of potential. It may reveal a purely artistic potential, but could also appear in subjects such as computing and systems, technology, and geography. If accompanied by verbal ability, you may well be drawn to careers where you can be involved with ideas and cultural activities, such as writing or media work.

# Chapter 6
# Three-D test

In this test you are asked to discover the hidden sides of objects. You are shown a stack of blocks. Each block is exactly the same size. You can see the front, or facing, sides. You can also see the top side. But you cannot see the two sides that are hidden from your view. Nor can you see the bottom, or underneath, side. However, you can imagine what the hidden sides and underneath must look like.

In the example on the next page, there is a stack of five blocks. You have to imagine, out of the five possibilities you are given, which one is the view from side A. Only one of the five is correct. Then, do the same for sides B and C. In each set of possibilities, only one is correct, even though it may have been turned around. Tick the correct one.

## Example

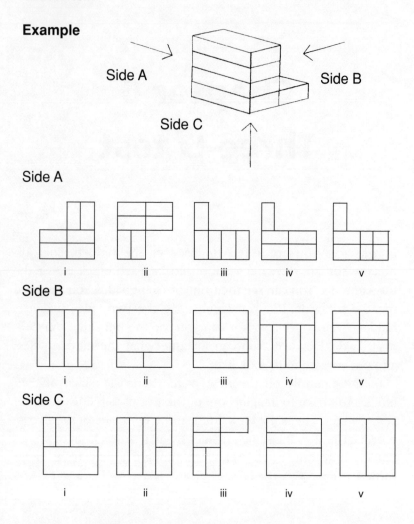

Side A

|     |     |     |     |     |
| --- | --- | --- | --- | --- |
| i   | ii  | iii | iv  | v   |

Side B

|     |     |     |     |     |
| --- | --- | --- | --- | --- |
| i   | ii  | iii | iv  | v   |

Side C

|     |     |     |     |     |
| --- | --- | --- | --- | --- |
| i   | ii  | iii | iv  | v   |

For the example, the answer is number iii for side A, even though it has been turned around. For side B, number i is the correct answer. Number v is the correct answer for side C.

You may find it helpful to have spare paper available. For each example, tick the correct choice out of the five options given for each side. Be careful, as the view may have been turned around. You have five minutes to do as many as you can.

**1.**

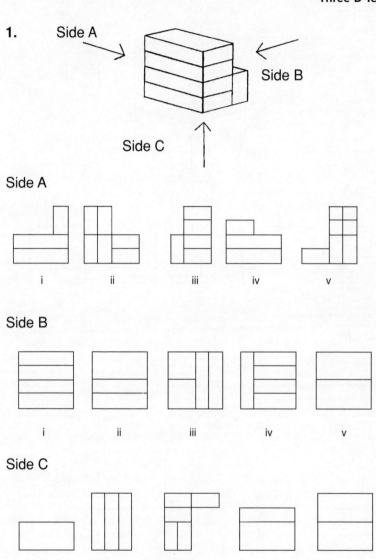

Side A

|     |     |     |     |     |
|-----|-----|-----|-----|-----|
| i   | ii  | iii | iv  | v   |

Side B

|     |     |     |     |     |
|-----|-----|-----|-----|-----|
| i   | ii  | iii | iv  | v   |

Side C

|     |     |     |     |     |
|-----|-----|-----|-----|-----|
| i   | ii  | iii | iv  | v   |

**2.**

Side A

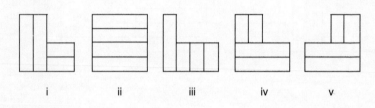

i ii iii iv v

Side B

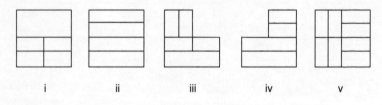

i ii iii iv v

Side C

i ii iii iv v

**3.**

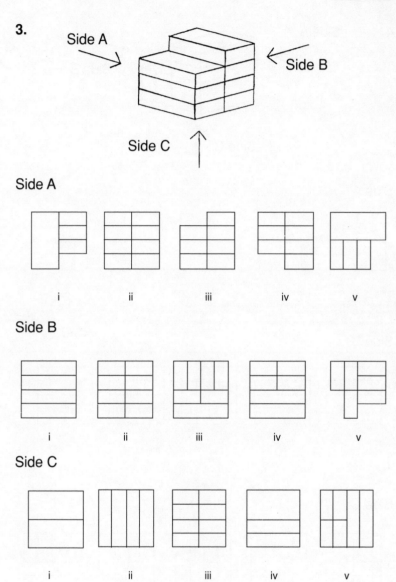

Side A

i  ii  iii  iv  v

Side B

i  ii  iii  iv  v

Side C

i  ii  iii  iv  v

**Test Yourself!**

**4.**

Side A

i      ii      iii      iv      v

Side B

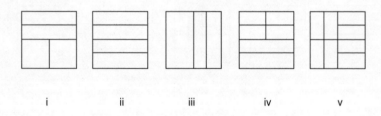

i      ii      iii      iv      v

Side C

i      ii      iii      iv      v

**5.**

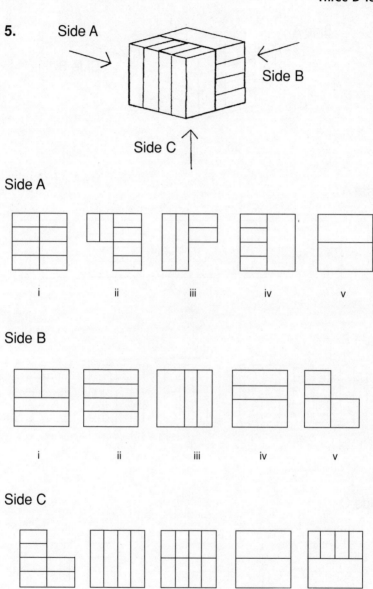

Side A

i  ii  iii  iv  v

Side B

i  ii  iii  iv  v

Side C

i  ii  iii  iv  v

**Test Yourself!**

**6.**

Side A

|   |   |   |   |   |
|---|---|---|---|---|
| i | ii | iii | iv | v |

Side B

|   |   |   |   |   |
|---|---|---|---|---|
| i | ii | iii | iv | v |

Side C

|   |   |   |   |   |
|---|---|---|---|---|
| i | ii | iii | iv | v |

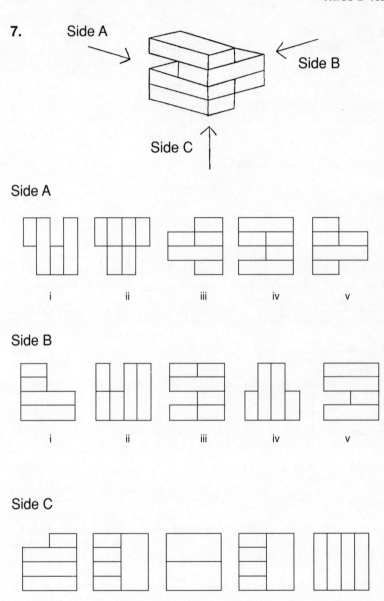

**7.**

Side A

Side B

Side C

Side A

i   ii   iii   iv   v

Side B

i   ii   iii   iv   v

Side C

i   ii   iii   iv   v

**8.**

Side A

| i | ii | iii | iv | v |

Side B

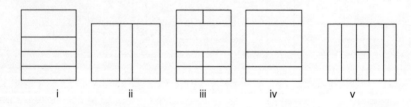

| i | ii | iii | iv | v |

Side C

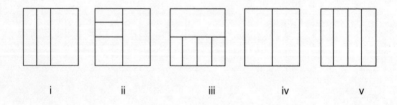

| i | ii | iii | iv | v |

**9.**

Side A

i    ii    iii    iv    v

Side B

i    ii    iii    iv    v

Side C

i    ii    iii    iv    v

**10.**

Side A

Side B

Side C

# Answers to three-D test

| 1 | A– iii | B – ii | C – iv |
|----|--------|---------|---------|
| 2 | A – iv | B – iii | C – v |
| 3 | A – iv | B – i | C – i |
| 4 | A – ii | B – iii | C – ii |
| 5 | A – iv | B – ii | C – v |
| 6 | A – i | B – iii | C– iii |
| 7 | A – v | B – v | C – iii |
| 8 | A – ii | B – iv | C– iv |
| 9 | A – v | B – iv | C – i |
| 10 | A – iii | B – iii | C – v |

## Obtaining the total score

| | number correct = | _____ | |
|---|---|---|---|
| | plus 3 if no mistakes | +3 _____ | |
| | Total score = | _____ | |

## Establishing level of potential

| average | above average | well above average | exceptional |
|---------|---------------|--------------------|-------------|
| 1–12 | 13–16 | 17–21 | 22+ |

## Interpretation

This test demands many of the same attributes as the test of spatial recognition. However, it does not distort the shapes in the same way, and the shapes themselves are regular.

Though the three-D is often an indicator of creative potential in the same way as the spatial recognition tests, it is usually predictive of success in areas that are more formal and require a more structured, technical approach, as in architecture and many forms of planning, for example.

This test is also different from the spatial recognition test, because the objects are specifically three-dimensional, not flat. This has implications for the way you think. Psychologically, it requires that you are able to 'look behind what appears on the surface of things'. You have to form a representation in your mind of what is on the other side. Literally, you have to conceive a diagram or picture that exists nowhere but in your own mind, which you infer from the original presented to you.

Possibly because the test demands that you bring an image together in your mind to form a unified whole, it was once thought that this type of test was the purest measure of intelligence. There is no doubt that it is another good measure of hard, natural intelligence. It will come to the surface in some way, even though it is not accompanied by the more formal verbal, numerical or visual aptitudes. People who have this type of potential are almost always recognized as intelligent, even though they may not necessarily do as well as expected in educational settings; they often do better when they have left formal schooling.

However, this aptitude by itself may express itself in design, drawing and craft skills. With numerical reasoning it would suggest professional training in areas connected with engineering and technology.

# Chapter 7
# Systems test

In this test you are given a series of letters and symbols at the top of each page. Each letter goes with a particular symbol. The letter is in the top box of each pair and the symbol is at the bottom.

Your task is to write in the letter that goes with each symbol. The example below shows you how. The first nine have been done already. Complete the last three yourself.

## Example

| A | B | C | D | E | F | G | H | I | J | K | L |
|---|---|---|---|---|---|---|---|---|---|---|---|
| ✈ | ⚵ | ☜ | 🕯 | ❄ | ✡ | ✝ | ✋ | ⚑ | 💣 | ☯ | ☪ |

## Example answer

| 1 | 2 | 3 | 4 | 5 | 6 | 7 | 8 | 9 | 10 | 11 | 12 |
|---|---|---|---|---|---|---|---|---|----|----|----|

| D | G | J | H | D | F | A | K | C |  |  |  |
|---|---|---|---|---|---|---|---|---|---|---|---|
| 🕯 | ✝ | 💣 | ✋ | 🕯 | ✡ | ✈ | ☯ | ☜ | 🕯 | ✈ | ⚵ |

The answers to 10, 11 and 12 are D, A and B.

**Test Yourself!**

On each page, look at the symbols that go with each letter at the top of the page. Then write in the missing letter that goes with each symbol for each of the test items. It is important to go as quickly as possible without making mistakes. You have exactly four minutes and you must get as many correct as possible in the time allowed.

| A | B | C | D | E | F | G | H | I | J | K | L |
|---|---|---|---|---|---|---|---|---|---|---|---|
| ✈ | ☦ | ☜ | 🕯 | ❄ | ✡ | ✝ | ✋ | ⚑ | 💣 | ☯ | ☪ |

| 1 | 2 | 3 | 4 | 5 | 6 | 7 | 8 | 9 | 10 | 11 | 12 |
|---|---|---|---|---|---|---|---|---|---|---|---|
| ☪ | ✈ | 💣 | ✋ | ⚑ | ❄ | ✈ | ✋ | ☪ | ☦ | ✈ | 🕯 |

| 13 | 14 | 15 | 16 | 17 | 18 | 19 | 20 | 21 | 22 | 23 | 24 |
|---|---|---|---|---|---|---|---|---|---|---|---|
| ⚑ | ✋ | 🕯 | ☯ | ⚑ | ✡ | ☪ | ☜ | ⚑ | ☦ | ❄ | ✡ |

| 25 | 26 | 27 | 28 | 29 | 30 | 31 | 32 | 33 | 34 | 35 | 36 |
|---|---|---|---|---|---|---|---|---|---|---|---|
| ☪ | ☯ | ☜ | ✡ | ☪ | ✈ | ⚑ | ❄ | ✝ | ✋ | 💣 | ✈ |

| 37 | 38 | 39 | 40 | 41 | 42 | 43 | 44 | 45 | 46 | 47 | 48 |
|---|---|---|---|---|---|---|---|---|---|---|---|
| ✡ | 💣 | ✝ | ☪ | 🕯 | ☦ | ☯ | 💣 | ❄ | ✡ | 🕯 | ☜ |

| 49 | 50 | 51 | 52 | 53 | 54 | 55 | 56 | 57 | 58 | 59 | 60 |
|---|---|---|---|---|---|---|---|---|---|---|---|
| ☯ | ❄ | ⚑ | 🕯 | ☯ | ✡ | ✈ | ☜ | ✝ | ☪ | 💣 | ✝ |

# Test Yourself!

| A | B | C | D | E | F | G | H | I | J | K | L |
|---|---|---|---|---|---|---|---|---|---|---|---|
| ✈ | ⚙ | ☞ | 🕯 | ❄ | ✡ | ✝ | ✋ | 🏴 | 💣 | ☯ | ☾★ |

| 61 | 62 | 63 | 64 | 65 | 66 | 67 | 68 | 69 | 70 | 71 | 72 |
|----|----|----|----|----|----|----|----|----|----|----|----|
| ✝ | ✡ | ✋ | ☯ | ☯ | ⚙ | 💣 | 🕯 | ☾★ | ✝ | ✈ | ☞ |

| 73 | 74 | 75 | 76 | 77 | 78 | 79 | 80 | 81 | 82 | 83 | 84 |
|----|----|----|----|----|----|----|----|----|----|----|----|
| 🕯 | ✋ | ✝ | 🏴 | ⚙ | ☾★ | ☯ | ❄ | ☾★ | 🏴 | ✡ | 🕯 |

| 85 | 86 | 87 | 88 | 89 | 90 | 91 | 92 | 93 | 94 | 95 | 96 |
|----|----|----|----|----|----|----|----|----|----|----|----|
| ✡ | 💣 | ✈ | ✋ | ☾★ | ☯ | ❄ | ✈ | ⚙ | ✋ | 🕯 | ✝ |

| 97 | 98 | 99 | 100 | 101 | 102 | 103 | 104 | 105 | 106 | 107 | 108 |
|----|----|----|-----|-----|-----|-----|-----|-----|-----|-----|-----|
| ✋ | ✡ | 🏴 | ⚙ | ☾★ | 🕯 | 🏴 | ☾★ | ✈ | ⚙ | 💣 | ✋ |

| 109 | 110 | 111 | 112 | 113 | 114 | 115 | 116 | 117 | 118 | 119 | 120 |
|-----|-----|-----|-----|-----|-----|-----|-----|-----|-----|-----|-----|
| ☯ | 💣 | ⚙ | ✈ | ✝ | 🏴 | ❄ | 💣 | ✋ | ✡ | 🕯 | ✝ |

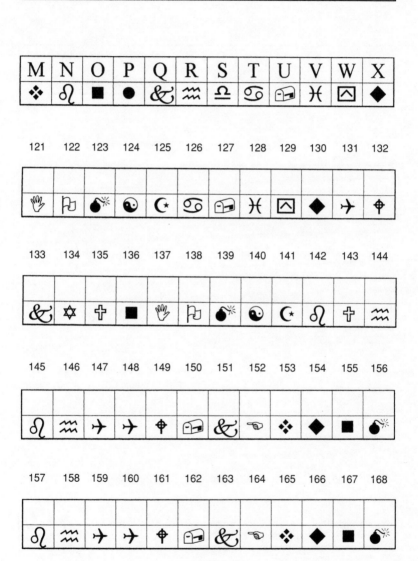

**Test Yourself!**

| A | B | C | D | E | F | G | H | I | J | K | L |
|---|---|---|---|---|---|---|---|---|---|---|---|
| ✈ | ☥ | ☞ | 🕯 | ❄ | ✡ | ✝ | ✋ | ⚑ | 💣 | ☯ | ☪ |

| M | N | O | P | Q | R | S | T | U | V | W | X |
|---|---|---|---|---|---|---|---|---|---|---|---|
| ❖ | ♌ | ■ | ● | & | ♒ | ♎ | ♋ | 📫 | ♓ | ⌂ | ◆ |

| 169 | 170 | 171 | 172 | 173 | 174 | 175 | 176 | 177 | 178 | 179 | 180 |
|---|---|---|---|---|---|---|---|---|---|---|---|
| & | ☪ | ♒ | 📫 | ♌ | & | ■ | ⚑ | 💣 | ✡ | ✋ | ♎ |

| 181 | 182 | 183 | 184 | 185 | 186 | 187 | 188 | 189 | 190 | 191 | 192 |
|---|---|---|---|---|---|---|---|---|---|---|---|
| ◆ | ✡ | ✝ | ✋ | ■ | ✈ | ☪ | 🕯 | ❄ | & | ❖ | ☞ |

| 193 | 194 | 195 | 196 | 197 | 198 | 199 | 200 | 201 | 202 | 203 | 204 |
|---|---|---|---|---|---|---|---|---|---|---|---|
| 📫 | ♌ | ♎ | ☞ | ❖ | ☪ | ◆ | ♒ | ✋ | ⚑ | 💣 | ■ |

| 205 | 206 | 207 | 208 | 209 | 210 | 211 | 212 | 213 | 214 | 215 | 216 |
|---|---|---|---|---|---|---|---|---|---|---|---|
| ◆ | ❖ | ☞ | 📫 | ♎ | ✈ | ☞ | 🕯 | ☪ | 🕯 | ❄ | ♒ |

# Answers to systems test

It is rare for people to make more than the odd or occasional mistake on this test. You can check, if you wish, for absolute accuracy, but the number of items you have attempted is likely to provide a reliable overall answer. If, however, you think you may have been guessing, and have therefore probably made some mistakes, you should go back and check what you have done, and take the number of errors you have made away from the number attempted.

## Obtaining the total score

| | number correct = | |
|---|---|---|
| | _____ | |

## Establishing level of potential

| average | above average | well above average | exceptional |
|---|---|---|---|
| 1–100 | 101–132 | 133–165 | 166+ |

## Interpretation

This is a demanding test because it can become tedious while at the same time demanding absolute concentration.

The way you attempted the test can be revealing. Most people check off symbols one by one as they appear. A variant of this approach is to take one symbol at a time, checking off all the same symbols on the page. If you have approached the test in one of these ways you are measuring your aptitude for checking and organization.

Another method is more conceptual, involving memorizing each one of the items as they become familiar. In this process the letter becomes identified with the symbol and takes its place. People who use this method eventually are quick on this test because they eliminate the time required for checking. If you made use of this method you are also measuring your aptitude for the memorization and recognition of information .

This aptitude is essential where attention to detail is required, as in many administrative situations. However, people who use the 'memory approach' may be at a disadvantage if they are presented with constantly new information to check, because this gives them no opportunity to form a concept they can retain in their memory to help them. They come into their own in dealing with information where they are expected to impose some sort of system or conceptual framework upon the information. In other words, they may be more adept at sorting out problems of order rather than checking the correctness of items.

Precision is usually appreciated in careers involving financial transactions and in legal work. The same type of ability is demanded in computer programming and analysis.

# Chapter 8
# Vocabulary test

This is a test of your understanding of words. You are given a word and have to say which one of the alternatives is closest in meaning to it. You have to place a tick in the correct box. Look at the examples below.

## Examples

| 1. OWN | | 2. ADD | |
|---|---|---|---|
| ☑ | a) possess | ☐ | a) subtract |
| ☐ | b) unpaid | ☑ | b) count |
| ☐ | c) disown | ☐ | c) duke |
| ☐ | d) landlord | ☐ | d) new |

In example Example 1, to *possess* means the same as to *own*. If you think of a sentence with the word *own* in it, you will find that the word *possess* could replace it. For example, 'I *own* a car – I *possess* a car.' *Unpaid* means owing, not to *own*. *Disown* means the opposite of to *own*. *Landlord* means an owner, not to *own*. *Own* and *possess* are verbs, while *unpaid* is an adjective, *disown* is a verb, but means the opposite of *own*; and *landlord* is a noun.

## Test Yourself!

In Example 2, *subtract* is the opposite of *add*, although it is a verb, as *add* is a verb. *Duke* is a noun, but does not mean *add*. *New* means fresh, and therefore could be added, but it would not be able to replace the word *add* in a sentence. In any case, fresh is an adjective. Both *add* and *count* are verbs. *Count* is the answer, because it is almost identical in meaning to add and could easily replace it in a sentence, for example, 'You should ADD up your money – You should count up your money.' It does not matter that *count* can have other meanings, for example, as a noun in 'The Count and Countess were invited to the palace.'

You can have as much time as you want to do this test, but it is probably not worth spending any longer than five minutes, as you will find that you either know the meanings of the words, or you do not.

Place a tick in the box of the alternative that is closest in meaning to the word in capitals.

| 1. BAD | |
|---|---|
| ☐ | a) evil |
| ☐ | b) angel |
| ☐ | c) good |
| ☐ | d) ban |

| 2. WET | |
|---|---|
| ☐ | a) appetite |
| ☐ | b) strong |
| ☐ | c) watery |
| ☐ | d) dry |

| 3. CHIEF | |
|---|---|
| ☐ | a) mainly |
| ☐ | b) minor |
| ☐ | c) head |
| ☐ | d) unimportant |

| 4. CHOP | |
|---|---|
| ☐ | a) rough |
| ☐ | b) duty |
| ☐ | c) stormy |
| ☐ | d) divide |

| 5. SOFT | 6. GOWN |
|---|---|
| ☐ a) harsh | ☐ a) sack |
| ☐ b) undemanding | ☐ b) shout |
| ☐ c) contact | ☐ c) robe |
| ☐ d) comfort | ☐ d) about |

| 7. IMAGINARY | 8. ACTIVE |
|---|---|
| ☐ a) realistic | ☐ a) mobile |
| ☐ b) bleak | ☐ b) baffle |
| ☐ c) trance | ☐ c) rigid |
| ☐ d) dreamy | ☐ d) motion |

| 9. PIERCE | 10. INVALUABLE |
|---|---|
| ☐ a) puncture | ☐ a) worthless |
| ☐ b) stung | ☐ b) valuable |
| ☐ c) loud | ☐ c) variable |
| ☐ d) stabbing | ☐ d) cheap |

| 11. ADAPT | 12. IMPARTIAL |
|---|---|
| ☐ a) convert | ☐ a) connected |
| ☐ b) flexible | ☐ b) detached |
| ☐ c) inflexible | ☐ c) involved |
| ☐ d) transformation | ☐ d) unconcern |

| 13. REPUTABLE | 14. LIGHTEN |
|---|---|
| ☐ a) infamous | ☐ a) discover |
| ☐ b) supposed | ☐ b) darken |
| ☐ c) good | ☐ c) illumine |
| ☐ d) stature | ☐ d) weak |

| 15. GROUNDLESS | 16. FASTEN |
|---|---|
| ☐ a) justified | ☐ a) affix |
| ☐ b) background | ☐ b) untie |
| ☐ c) basis | ☐ c) holder |
| ☐ d) absurd | ☐ d) thin |

| 17. BARGAINING | 18. WORRISOME |
|---|---|
| ☐ a) trafficking | ☐ a) reassuring |
| ☐ b) anticipate | ☐ b) unworried |
| ☐ c) promise | ☐ c) annoy |
| ☐ d) agree | ☐ d) perturbing |

| 19. UNDERCURRENT | 20. SATANIC |
|---|---|
| ☐ a) undercharge | ☐ a) divine |
| ☐ b) atmosphere | ☐ b) devil |
| ☐ c) undermine | ☐ c) inhuman |
| ☐ d) belittle | ☐ d) biting |

| 21. PRICELESS | 22. MUTINOUS |
|---|---|
| ☐ a) prized | ☐ a) defiance |
| ☐ b) cheap | ☐ b) uprising |
| ☐ c) menu | ☐ c) obedient |
| ☐ d) expense | ☐ d) turbulent |

| 23. HOMELY | 24. FUNCTIONAL |
|---|---|
| ☐ a) mother | ☐ a) plain |
| ☐ b) domestic | ☐ b) official |
| ☐ c) formal | ☐ c) decorative |
| ☐ d) revered | ☐ d) gathering |

| 25. EXEMPT | 26. GALLANT |
|---|---|
| ☐ a) spared | ☐ a) cowardly |
| ☐ b) liable | ☐ b) escort |
| ☐ c) except | ☐ c) courageousness |
| ☐ d) illustrate | ☐ d) polite |

| 27. EXPRESSLY | 28. DAPPER |
|---|---|
| ☐ a) assert | ☐ a) sloppy |
| ☐ b) energetic | ☐ b) spry |
| ☐ c) particularly | ☐ c) bespeckled |
| ☐ d) vaguely | ☐ d) dappled |

| 29. COGNIZANT | 30. PORTEND |
|---|---|
| ☐ a) unaware | ☐ a) presage |
| ☐ b) apprehension | ☐ b) insignificant |
| ☐ c) acquainted | ☐ c) presentiment |
| ☐ d) perception | ☐ d) emblazon |

| 31. BENEDICTION | 32. CONCOMITANT |
|---|---|
| ☐ a) anathema | ☐ a) coincidental |
| ☐ b) benevolence | ☐ b) accidental |
| ☐ c) munificence | ☐ c) incidental |
| ☐ d) blessing | ☐ d) compressed |

| 33. GUILELESS | 34. CULMINATE |
|---|---|
| ☐ a) artful | ☐ a) crown |
| ☐ b) shame | ☐ b) peak |
| ☐ c) innocent | ☐ c) begin |
| ☐ d) transparent | ☐ d) pursue |

| 35. EXONERATE | 36. ICONOCLASTIC |
|---|---|
| ☐ a) absolution | ☐ a) denunciatory |
| ☐ b) inflate | ☐ b) credulity |
| ☐ c) incriminate | ☐ c) uncritical |
| ☐ d) vindicate | ☐ d) optimistic |

| 37. IMPLICIT | 38. PENURIOUS |
|---|---|
| ☐ a) innuendo | ☐ a) paucity |
| ☐ b) explicit | ☐ b) indigent |
| ☐ c) latent | ☐ c) dearth |
| ☐ d) stated | ☐ d) meditative |

| 39. SPURIOUS | 40. TRANSMOGRIFY |
|---|---|
| ☐ a) authentic | ☐ a) attitudinize |
| ☐ b) specious | ☐ b) traverse |
| ☐ c) sordid | ☐ c) mutation |
| ☐ d) dishevelled | ☐ d) metamorphose |

# Answers to vocabulary test

| | | | | |
|---|---|---|---|---|
| 1 – a | 9 – a | 17 – a | 25 – c | 33 – d |
| 2 – c | 10 – b | 18 – d | 26 – d | 34 – b |
| 3 – c | 11 – a | 19 – b | 27 – c | 35 – d |
| 4 – d | 12 – b | 20 – c | 28 – b | 36 – a |
| 5 – b | 13 – c | 21 – a | 29 – c | 37 – c |
| 6 – c | 14 – c | 22 – d | 30 – a | 38 – b |
| 7 – d | 15 – d | 23 – b | 31 – d | 39 – b |
| 8 – a | 16 – a | 24 – a | 32 – c | 40 – d |

## Obtaining the total score

| | number correct = | | |
|---|---|---|---|
| plus 4 if you are aged under 16 | plus 2 if aged 17–20 | + | |
| | Total score = | | |

## Establishing level of potential

| average | above average | well above average | exceptional |
|---|---|---|---|
| 1–19 | 20–25 | 26–30 | 31+ |

## Interpretation

The vocabulary test may be regarded as a test of knowledge like any learnt skill, and therefore different from the other tests, which look at more abstract, underlying potential. It is true that the vocabulary is not measuring innate intelligence, that is, what you were born with. However, it is measuring a means by which intelligence is choosing to express itself. Through the use of words, bearing in mind that words form concepts, there is scope for clear analysis and expression of information as well as abstract ideas. It is certainly an area of potential that is relevant to career success.

Lack of a strong vocabulary will probably not hold you back in your career, provided you have other areas of potential that are more important for the task or type of work on which you are engaged. It will obviously hold you back in areas of communication in which a high vocabulary is expected. Typically, students on technically oriented courses do less well on vocabulary tests than those who are pursuing arts courses such as English, history, languages or philosophy. All these demand that words be used correctly and precisely.

Although a comparatively weak vocabulary may not necessarily be essential to success, many people gain promotion to a level where they believe that lack of vocabulary is a serious disadvantage. If your vocabulary is lower than your other test scores, you can certainly take it that you have the potential to improve your vocabulary.

# Chapter 9
# Aptitude profiling and 'IQ'

## Level of score

'Average' means that you scored about as well as most other people on a test. Therefore, no especial aptitude has been detected on this occasion. You may have an aptitude for a type of problem solving that has not been detected by the specific test. It could be that the areas of work that may be predicted by this test may be less suited to you than those suggested by other tests where there is stronger evidence. Areas of work suggested by results providing the strongest evidence are the ones that will most likely be where you will find it easiest to be successful.

On page 108 you will find a chart titled 'Your aptitude profile'. Place your own scores in the chart by circling your own score in the appropriate place.

If you connect up the scores, you should have a graph that looks something like the example:

## Example profile

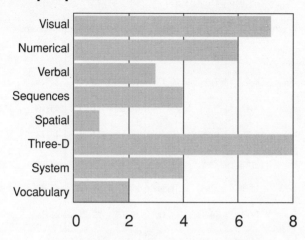

# Your aptitude profile

Mark the place where each of your test results falls in the chart. You can draw a bar from the left of the chart to your score, to form a bar line, as in the example profile above.

## Your aptitude profile

| Test | average | | above average | | well above average | | exceptional | |
|------|------|------|------|------|------|------|------|------|
| | 1 | 2 | 3 | 4 | 5 | 6 | 7 | 8 |
| VISUAL | 1-3 | 4-6 | 7-9 | 10-13 | 14-17 | 18-20 | 21-24 | 25+ |
| NUMERICAL | 1-2 | 3-4 | 5 | 6-7 | 8-10 | 11-12 | 13-16 | 17+ |
| VERBAL | 1-3 | 4-7 | 8-9 | 10-11 | 12-13 | 14-15 | 16-18 | 19+ |
| SEQUENCES | 1-4 | 5-8 | 9-10 | 11-12 | 13-16 | 17-18 | 19-21 | 22+ |
| SPATIAL | 1-12 | 13-26 | 27-30 | 31-34 | 35-38 | 39-42 | 43-48 | 49+ |
| THREE-D | 1-6 | 7-12 | 13-14 | 15-16 | 17-18 | 19-21 | 22-24 | 25+ |
| SYSTEMS | 1-50 | 51-100 | 101-116 | 117-132 | 133-149 | 150-165 | 166-183 | 184+ |
| VOCABULARY | 1-9 | 10-19 | 20-22 | 23-25 | 26-27 | 28-30 | 31-34 | 35+ |

# Differences between scores

Your profile readily enables you to see possible differences between your scores. These differences may not be significant. For example, on another occasion, your differences between scores might be reversed, so that on one occasion you seem to do better with verbal than with visual reasoning, but on the next occasion do better with visual reasoning than with verbal reasoning. This may be because you are really equally good on both tests. It may be that tiredness, or other reasons, affect your performance on different occasions.

However, the greater the difference between tests, the more likely it is that you really are better on one type of test than another. This difference may be important to you in determining the most suitable area of study or what career to pursue.

*(Read the following if your test scores are different from what you had assumed and if you disagree with the results.)*

*If you wish, there is no reason why you should not place your own estimates of your potential, if these are different from your test results, in the chart. It depends on how far you agree that the test results are fully and accurately assessing you. There is always room for some doubt. As discussed in the Introduction, your results on the tests might be affected by all sorts of issues relating to:*

■ *the efficiency with which you test yourself;*

■ *the conditions in which you test yourself;*

■ *who you compare yourself with; and*

■ *whether the tests themselves have reliably detected your potential.*

*Therefore, your own estimates might be based upon your progress at school and upon other experiences.*

As a rough guide, take it that if there is a clear section between two scores, there may be a significant difference in your aptitude. For example, if your score on one test is in the upper section of good evidence and another score is in the upper part of some evidence, there will be a section (clear score area) between the two scores. You can become more certain, the more sections there are between the two scores. To make this clear, each of your scores on the tests will fall under a number 1–8 written in the chart at the top. So, for example, there may not be any real difference between a score of 5 and 6, but there is likely to be a real difference in your potential if the scores are 5 and 7. The greater the difference between scores, the greater the difference in your potential. How much weight you place upon the difference between any two scores is, in the end, for you to judge.

Interpretation of your profile is reasonably easy if you have one result that stands out from the others. There remains the difficulty of relating this aptitude to a career – even a distinct aptitude may translate into numerous career options.

Most people will obtain a pattern where there is no single, distinguishable aptitude, but rather a pattern that appears to consist of relative 'highs and lows'. Your highest score might be the best indication, but also look at any other relatively high scores.

Do your scores seem to group themselves in any way? How are your high scores different from your lower scores? What, broadly, do the relative highs and lows tell you? Some people do better with all the word and numerical types of test, but not visual types and spatial types. This would be interpreted as more of an administrative as opposed to an artistic pattern. Others may do well on both the numerical and visual tests, but not so well on the verbal side. This might indicate more of a scientific bias. There are, of course, many possible patterns for you to interpret.

The level of the various scores is not particularly relevant and you may have other high scores besides those that are frequently indicative of potential in certain areas. Your own pattern is most unlikely to be identical to the following common patterns, but you may find them useful for general guidance.

# Aptitude profiles and courses of study

## Accountancy and finance

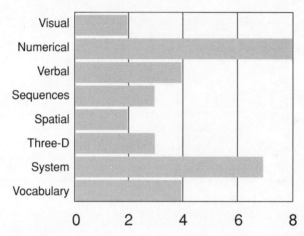

## Agriculture and land management

# Archaeology and anthropology

# Architecture

# Art and design

# Art history

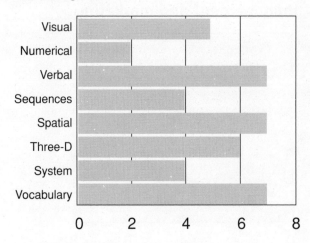

# Biology and the biological sciences

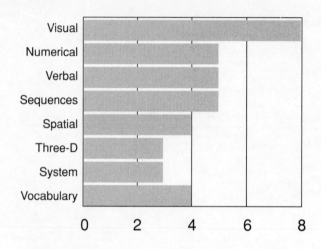

# Business, management and marketing

# Catering

# Chemistry

# Classics

# Computing and IT

# Craft

# Dance

# Drama

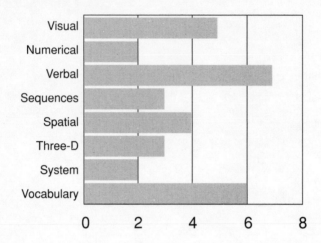

# Ecology and environmental sciences

## Economics

## Engineering

# English

# Fashion

# Geography

# History

# Hotel management

# Languages and linguistics

# Law

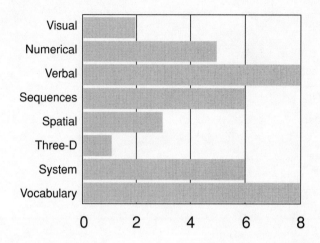

# Library and information science

## Mathematics and statistics

## Media and communication

# Music

# Nursing

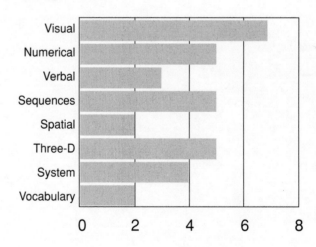

# Philosophy and religious studies

# Physics

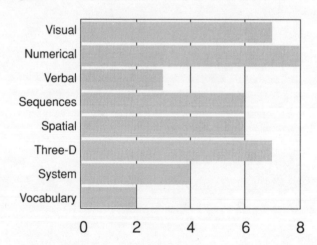

# Politics and international relations

# Psychology

# Sociology

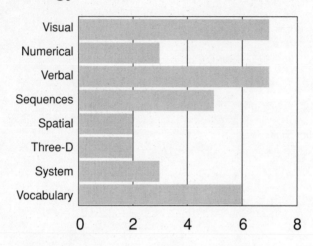

# Sport and leisure studies

# Textile technology

# Veterinary medicine

# IQ

Your IQ (intelligence quotient) is a number by which you can compare yourself with other people. In an indirect way, you have already been doing this with your test results in this book. All that an IQ does is attempt to give you more precise information as to where you stand on the comparative scale.

This book cannot measure your IQ with any great accuracy, as the conditions for measuring your IQ, as well as the information required to compare your intelligence with a satisfactory sample of people like you, are not available.

Why then, provide a guide to IQ? Because many people find the exercise interesting for its own sake. And because the tests in this book are very similar to other tests used to measure intelligence, it enables a fuller comprehension of the entire process of intellectual measurement. Furthermore, an estimate of IQ provides a quick way of asking yourself whether you are going in a direction with your studies or in your career that will allow you to fully use your potential.

## Intelligence tests

These are designed to assess innate qualities as far as possible uncontaminated by learning. This is why so many intelligence tests seem to be so abstract and unrelated to what we usually do. In practice, it is very difficult indeed to assess intelligence without using words, figures or shapes that have at least some familiarity to you. The other side to this equation is that the whole point of measuring IQ is to see whether a person has intelligence that has not yet been developed. It thus provides a measure of how much more a person could achieve, if circumstances could be arranged to permit realization of that person's innate potential.

Aptitude tests may be slightly different from intelligence tests, because they are designed to assess potential for something specific. For example, rather than assess to what degree a person may be able to think through problems, aptitude tests attempt to assess whether a person can think through problems that are relevant to distinct fields of endeavour. What distinguishes aptitude tests from intelligence tests is that the purpose of aptitude tests is more practical.

# The IQ scale

Most IQ scales use the number 100 as an average. People with above average scores, say, up to about 115 on appropriate tests, usually extend their schooling, obtaining vocational and technical qualifications.

People with stronger aptitudes are usually able to apply themselves to degree or professional courses. This group will, roughly, be the intellectual top 10 per cent and have an average IQ of 119.

The top 5 per cent have an IQ around 125. If you are very good at the tests, you may have an IQ of around 135, which puts you into the top 1 per cent.

Remember to interpret your own score only as a general guide. If we assume that you might have a 'true' IQ this will not be revealed unless you are compared with people of the same age, sex and relevant background. It is best to assume that your own IQ from the table provided here is likely to be only a baseline estimate. Use it to ask yourself whether you are achieving what you would expect at college or in your career. What tests should you use to calculate your IQ? It is possible to obtain an

IQ on each one of the tests. The fairest estimate is probably to take the sum of several scores, then divide that number by the number of tests you have used.

# Your IQ

|  | 100 | 105 | 110 | 115 | 120 | 125 | 130 | 135 | 140 | 145 |
|---|---|---|---|---|---|---|---|---|---|---|
| VISUAL | 1-6 | 7-9 | 10-13 | 14-17 | 18-20 | 21-24 | 25-26 | 27-28 | 29-30 | 31-32 |
| NUMERICAL | 1-4 | 5 | 6-7 | 8-10 | 11-12 | 13-16 | 17-18 | 19 | 20 | 21 |
| VERBAL | 1-7 | 8-9 | 10-11 | 12-13 | 14-15 | 16-18 | 19-20 | 21-22 | 23-26 | 27-33 |
| SEQUENCES | 1-8 | 9-10 | 11-12 | 13-16 | 17-18 | 19-21 | 22-24 | 25-28 | 29-30 | 31-32 |
| SPATIAL | 1-26 | 27-30 | 31-34 | 35-38 | 39-42 | 43-48 | 49-54 | 55-60 | 61-65 | 66-70 |
| THREE-D | 1-12 | 13-14 | 15-16 | 17-18 | 19-21 | 22-24 | 25-26 | 27-28 | 29 | 30 |
| SYSTEMS | 1-100 | 101-116 | 117-132 | 133-149 | 150-165 | 166-183 | 184-200 | 201-208 | 209-214 | 215-218 |
| VOCABULARY | 1-19 | 20-22 | 23-25 | 26-27 | 28-30 | 31-34 | 35-36 | 37-38 | 39 | 40 |

## Calculating your 'IQ'

('X' equals the number of tests used.)

Total 'IQ/' score
from X tests          = _____

Divide by X tests     / _____

'IQ'                  = _____

# Aptitudes and career profiles

Code
V     Visual
N     Numerical
Ve    Verbal
S     Sequential
Sp    Spatial
3D    Three-D
Sy    Systems
Vo    Vocabulary

Note: Where it has been considered that a career may be suitable on the basis of aptitude on any of the tests, no tricks have been placed.

| | V | N | Ve | S | Sp | 3D | Sy | Vo |
|---|---|---|---|---|---|---|---|---|
| Accident assessor | | | ✔ | | ✔ | ✔ | | |
| Accountant | | ✔ | | | | | ✔ | |
| Accounting technician | | ✔ | | | | | ✔ | |
| Actor | | | ✔ | | | | | ✔ |
| Actuary | ✔ | ✔ | | ✔ | | | ✔ | |
| Acupuncturist | ✔ | | | | ✔ | | | |
| Administrator | | | | | | | ✔ | ✔ |
| Advertising copywriter | | | ✔ | | | | | ✔ |
| Advertising executive | | ✔ | ✔ | ✔ | ✔ | | | ✔ |
| Aerobics instructor | | | | | ✔ | | | |
| Aeronautical engineer | ✔ | ✔ | | | ✔ | ✔ | | |
| Aeronautical technician | | ✔ | | | | ✔ | | |
| Agricultural mechanic | | | ✔ | | ✔ | | | |
| Agricultural secretary | | | | | | | ✔ | |
| Agriculturalist | | ✔ | | | ✔ | | | |
| Airline cabin staff | | | | | | | ✔ | |
| Air traffic controller | ✔ | ✔ | | ✔ | | | | |
| Ambulance crew | | | | | | | | |
| Anaesthetist | ✔ | ✔ | | | | | | |
| Animal keeper | | | | | | | | |
| Animal nurse | | | | | | | | |
| Anthropologist | ✔ | | ✔ | ✔ | | | | |

133

**Test Yourself!**

| | V | N | Ve | S | Sp | 3D | Sy | Vo |
|---|---|---|---|---|---|---|---|---|
| Antique dealer | | | | | ✔ | | | |
| Appliance repairer | | | | | ✔ | ✔ | | |
| Arborist | | | | | ✔ | | | |
| Aromatherapist | ✔ | | | | | | | |
| Architect | ✔ | ✔ | | | ✔ | ✔ | | |
| Architectural technician | ✔ | | | | ✔ | ✔ | | |
| Archivist | | | ✔ | | | | ✔ | ✔ |
| Armed forces officer | ✔ | ✔ | | | | | | |
| Armed forces personnel | | | | | | | | |
| Art dealer | | | | | ✔ | | | |
| Art restorer | | | | | ✔ | | | |
| Art therapist | | | | | ✔ | | | |
| Artist | | | | | ✔ | | | |
| Arts adminstrator | | ✔ | | | | | ✔ | |
| Astronaut | ✔ | ✔ | | | | | ✔ | |
| Atronomer | ✔ | ✔ | | | ✔ | | | |
| Auctioneer | | | | | ✔ | | | |
| Audiology technician | ✔ | | | | | ✔ | | |
| Auditor | | ✔ | | ✔ | | | ✔ | |
| Author | | | ✔ | | | | | ✔ |
| Automobile technician | | | | | ✔ | ✔ | | |
| | | | | | | | | |
| Bacteriologist | ✔ | ✔ | | | | | ✔ | |
| Baggage handler | | | | | | | | |
| Baker | | | | | | | | |
| Ballet dancer | | | | | ✔ | | | |
| Bank clerk | | ✔ | | | | | ✔ | |
| Bank manager | | ✔ | | | | | ✔ | |
| Barperson | | | | | | | | |
| Barrister | | ✔ | ✔ | | | | | ✔ |
| Beautician | | | | | ✔ | | | |
| Bicycle repairer | | | | | | ✔ | | |
| Bilingual secretary | | | ✔ | | | | ✔ | ✔ |
| Biologist | ✔ | ✔ | | | | | | |
| Biomedical engineer | | ✔ | | | | ✔ | | |
| Blacksmith/farrier | | | | | ✔ | | | |
| Boat builder | | | | | ✔ | ✔ | | |

134

|                              | V | N | Ve | S | Sp | 3D | Sy | Vo |
|------------------------------|---|---|----|---|----|----|----|----|
| Bookbinder                   |   |   |    |   |    | ✔  |    |    |
| Book critic                  |   |   | ✔  |   |    |    |    | ✔  |
| Book illustrator             |   |   |    |   |    |    |    |    |
| Bookseller                   |   | ✔ |    |   | ✔  |    |    |    |
| Botanist                     | ✔ |   |    |   |    |    |    |    |
| Brewer                       |   |   |    |   |    |    |    |    |
| Bricklayer                   |   |   |    |   |    | ✔  |    |    |
| Broker                       |   | ✔ |    |   |    |    |    |    |
| Builder's merchant           |   | ✔ |    |   |    |    |    |    |
| Building demolition expert   |   |   | ✔  | ✔ |    |    |    |    |
| Building inspector           |   |   |    |   |    | ✔  |    |    |
| Building society assistant   |   | ✔ |    |   |    |    | ✔  |    |
| Building society manager     |   | ✔ |    |   |    |    | ✔  |    |
| Building surveyor            |   |   |    |   | ✔  | ✔  |    |    |
| Bursar                       |   | ✔ |    |   |    |    |    |    |
| Bus driver                   |   |   |    |   |    |    |    |    |
| Business consultant          |   | ✔ |    | ✔ |    |    |    |    |
| Buyer                        |   | ✔ |    |   | ✔  |    | ✔  |    |
|                              |   |   |    |   |    |    |    |    |
| Cabinet maker                |   |   |    |   | ✔  |    |    |    |
| Camera repairer              |   |   |    |   |    | ✔  |    |    |
| Car body designer            |   |   |    |   | ✔  |    |    |    |
| Careers adviser              |   |   |    |   |    |    |    |    |
| Carpenter                    |   |   |    |   |    | ✔  |    |    |
| Cartographer                 |   |   |    |   | ✔  |    | ✔  |    |
| Cartoon animator             |   |   |    |   | ✔  |    |    |    |
| Cashier                      |   | ✔ |    |   |    |    | ✔  |    |
| Caterer                      |   |   |    |   | ✔  |    |    |    |
| CD-ROM producer              |   | ✔ |    |   | ✔  |    |    |    |
| Chef                         | ✔ |   |    |   | ✔  |    |    |    |
| Chemical technician          | ✔ |   |    |   |    |    |    |    |
| Chemical technologist        | ✔ | ✔ |    |   |    |    |    |    |
| Chemist                      | ✔ | ✔ |    |   |    |    | ✔  |    |
| Chief executive              |   | ✔ | ✔  | ✔ |    |    |    | ✔  |
| Child care worker            |   |   |    |   |    |    |    |    |
| Chimney sweep                | ✔ |   |    |   |    | ✔  |    |    |
| Chiropodist                  | ✔ |   |    |   |    | ✔  |    |    |

**Test Yourself!**

| | V | N | Ve | S | Sp | 3D | Sy | Vo |
|---|---|---|---|---|---|---|---|---|
| Choreographer | | | | | ✔ | | | |
| Cinema manager | | | | | | | | |
| Civil engineer | | ✔ | | | | ✔ | | |
| Civil servant | | ✔ | ✔ | | | | ✔ | ✔ |
| Clerk | | | | | | | ✔ | |
| Clinical psychologist | ✔ | ✔ | ✔ | ✔ | | | | |
| Clown | | | | | ✔ | | | |
| Club manager | | | | | | | | |
| Coastguard | | | | | | | | |
| College admissions counsellor | | | | | | | ✔ | |
| Comic illustrator | | | | | ✔ | | | |
| Commercial account manager | | ✔ | | | | | ✔ | |
| Community social worker | | | | | | | | |
| Community warden | | | | | | | | |
| Company secretary | | ✔ | | | | | ✔ | ✔ |
| Compositor | | | | | | ✔ | | |
| Computer animator | | ✔ | | | | | | |
| Computer game designer | ✔ | | | | ✔ | ✔ | ✔ | |
| Computer hardware designer | | ✔ | | | ✔ | ✔ | | |
| Computer systems analyst | ✔ | | | ✔ | | | | |
| Computer technician | ✔ | | | ✔ | | | | |
| Confectioner | | | | | | | | |
| Conference organizer | | | | | | | | |
| Conservation officer | ✔ | | | | | | | |
| Copywriter | | | ✔ | | | | | ✔ |
| Coroner | ✔ | ✔ | | | | | | |
| Cost accountant | | ✔ | | | | | ✔ | |
| Counsellor | | | | | | | | |
| Courier | | | | | | | | |
| Court reporter | | | | | | | ✔ | ✔ |
| Crane operator | | | | | | | | |
| Criminologist | ✔ | | | ✔ | | | | |
| Cruise director | | | | | | | | |
| Cryptographer | ✔ | | | | ✔ | ✔ | ✔ | ✔ |
| Cultural anthropologist | ✔ | | ✔ | | | | | |
| Curator | | | ✔ | | ✔ | | | |
| Currency trader | | ✔ | | | | | | |

| | V | N | Ve | S | Sp | 3D | Sy | Vo |
|---|---|---|---|---|---|---|---|---|
| Customer services manager | | | | | | | | |
| Customs officer | | | | | | | | |
| | | | | | | | | |
| Dance instructor | | | | | | | | |
| Dancer | | | | | | | | |
| Deaf interpreter | | | | | | | | |
| Decorator | | | | | ✔ | | | |
| Demonstrator | | | | | | | | |
| Dental assistant | ✔ | | | | | | | |
| Dental hygienist | ✔ | | | | | | | |
| Dental nurse | ✔ | | | | | | | |
| Dental technician | ✔ | | | | | ✔ | | |
| Dentist | ✔ | ✔ | | | ✔ | ✔ | | |
| Dermatologist | ✔ | | | | | | | |
| Design engineer | | ✔ | | | | ✔ | | |
| Designer | | | | | ✔ | | | |
| Dietician | ✔ | | | | | ✔ | | |
| Director (media) | | | ✔ | ✔ | | | | ✔ |
| Disc jockey | | | | | | | | |
| Dispensing optician | ✔ | | | | | | | |
| Display artist | | | | | ✔ | | | |
| Diver | | | | | | ✔ | | |
| Doctor of medicine | ✔ | ✔ | | | | ✔ | ✔ | |
| Drama teacher | | | ✔ | | | | | ✔ |
| Draughtsperson | | ✔ | | | | ✔ | ✔ | |
| Dresser (stage) | | | | | ✔ | | | |
| Dressmaker | | | | | ✔ | | | |
| Driver | | | | | | | | |
| Drug and alcohol counsellor | | | | | | | | |
| Drycleaner | | | | | | | | |
| | | | | | | | | |
| Ecologist | ✔ | | | | | | | |
| Economist | | ✔ | ✔ | | | | | ✔ |
| Editor | | | ✔ | | | | ✔ | ✔ |
| Editor (newspapers) | | | ✔ | ✔ | | | ✔ | ✔ |
| Editorial cartoonist | | | ✔ | | ✔ | | | |
| Educational psychologist | ✔ | ✔ | ✔ | | | | | |

| | V | N | Ve | S | Sp | 3D | Sy | Vo |
|---|---|---|---|---|---|---|---|---|
| Electrical engineer | | ✔ | | | | ✔ | | |
| Electrician | | | | | | ✔ | | |
| Electronics engineer | ✔ | | | | | ✔ | | |
| Elementary school teacher | | | | | ✔ | | ✔ | ✔ |
| Embalmer | | | | ✔ | | | | |
| Employment officer | | | | | | | | |
| Engineering pattern maker | | ✔ | | | | ✔ | | |
| Engineering technician | | ✔ | | | | ✔ | | |
| English language teacher | | | ✔ | | | | | ✔ |
| Engraver | | | | | ✔ | | | |
| Entertainments officer | | | | | | | | |
| Environmental health officer | ✔ | | | | | | | |
| Equestrian | | ✔ | | | ✔ | ✔ | | |
| Ergonomist | | ✔ | | | ✔ | ✔ | | |
| Estate agent | | | | | | | | |
| Estate manager | | | | | | | | |
| Exhibition organizer | | | | | | | | |
| Explosives expert | ✔ | | | ✔ | ✔ | ✔ | ✔ | |
| | | | | | | | | |
| Farm manager | | ✔ | | | | ✔ | | |
| Farmer | | | | | | ✔ | | |
| Farmworker | | | | | ✔ | | | |
| Fashion buyer | | ✔ | | | ✔ | | | |
| Fashion designer | | | | | ✔ | | | |
| Film projectionist | | | | | | ✔ | | |
| Film reviewer | | | ✔ | | ✔ | | | ✔ |
| Financial analyst | | ✔ | | | | | ✔ | |
| Financial controller | | ✔ | | | | | ✔ | |
| Firefighter | | | | | | ✔ | | |
| Fisheries officer | | | | | | | | |
| Fisherman | | | | | | | | |
| Fitter | | | | | | ✔ | | |
| Flight attendant | | | | | | | | |
| Florist | | | | | ✔ | | | |
| Flyperson (theatre) | | | | | ✔ | | | |
| Food hygiene inspector | ✔ | | | | | | | |
| Food service worker | | | | | | | | |

| | V | N | Ve | S | Sp | 3D | Sy | Vo |
|---|---|---|---|---|---|---|---|---|
| Foreign correspondent | | | ✔ | | | | | ✔ |
| Foreign language teacher | | | ✔ | | | | | ✔ |
| Forensic pathologist | ✔ | ✔ | | | ✔ | ✔ | | |
| Forensic psychologist | ✔ | | | ✔ | | | | ✔ |
| Forensic scientist | ✔ | ✔ | | | ✔ | ✔ | | |
| Forester | | | | | | | | |
| Freelance writer | | | ✔ | | | | | ✔ |
| Fund raiser | | | | | | | | |
| Funeral director | | | | | | | | |
| Furniture maker | | ✔ | | | ✔ | | | |
| | | | | | | | | |
| Gamekeeper | | | | | | | | |
| Gardener | | | | | | | | |
| Genealogist | ✔ | | | | | | ✔ | |
| Geneticist | ✔ | ✔ | | | | | | |
| Geochemist | ✔ | ✔ | | | | | | |
| Geologist | | ✔ | | | ✔ | | | |
| Glassblower | | | | | | | | |
| Glazier | | | | | | ✔ | | |
| Golf professional | | | | | | | | |
| Graphic designer | | | | | ✔ | | | |
| Grocer | | | | | | | | |
| Groundsperson | | | | | | | | |
| Guard | | | | | | | | |
| Gunsmith | | | | | ✔ | ✔ | | |
| | | | | | | | | |
| Hairdresser | | | | | ✔ | | | |
| Head teacher | ✔ | ✔ | ✔ | ✔ | | | | ✔ |
| Health services administrator | | | | | | | ✔ | |
| Health visitor | ✔ | | | | | | | |
| Heating engineer | | | | | | ✔ | | |
| Historian | | | ✔ | | | | | ✔ |
| Homeopath | ✔ | | | | | | | |
| Horologist | | | | | | | | |
| Horticulturalist | | ✔ | | | | ✔ | | |
| Hospital physicist | ✔ | ✔ | | ✔ | | ✔ | | |
| Hospital porter | | | | | | | | |

**Test Yourself!**

| | V | N | Ve | S | Sp | 3D | Sy | Vo |
|---|---|---|---|---|---|---|---|---|
| Hostel warden | | | | | | | | |
| Hotel manager | | ✓ | | | ✓ | | | |
| House parent | | | | | | | | |
| Housing manager | | | | | | | ✓ | |
| Human resources manager | | | ✓ | | | | ✓ | ✓ |
| Hydrographic surveyor | ✓ | | | | | ✓ | | |
| Hydrologist | ✓ | | | | | ✓ | | |
| | | | | | | | | |
| Illustrator | | | | | ✓ | | | |
| Immunologist | ✓ | ✓ | | | | | | |
| Importer/exporter | | ✓ | | | | | | |
| Industrial designer | | | | | ✓ | | | |
| Industrial nurse | ✓ | | | | | | | |
| Industrial relations officer | | | | | | | | |
| Information officer | | | | | | | | ✓ |
| Information scientist | ✓ | | | | | | | ✓ |
| Instrument and control engineer | ✓ | | | | ✓ | | | |
| Instrument maker | | | | | | ✓ | | |
| Insurance adjuster | ✓ | | | | | | ✓ | |
| Insurange agent | | | | | | | ✓ | |
| Interior designer | | | | | ✓ | | | |
| Interpreter | | | ✓ | | | | | |
| Interviewer | | | ✓ | | | | | |
| | | | | | | | | |
| Jewellery maker | | | | | ✓ | | | |
| Jockey | | | | | | | | |
| Joiner | | | | | | ✓ | | |
| Journalist | | | ✓ | | | | | ✓ |
| Judge | | | ✓ | ✓ | | | | ✓ |
| Justices clerk | | | | | | | ✓ | |
| | | | | | | | | |
| Laboratory technician | ✓ | | | | | ✓ | | |
| Landscape architect | ✓ | ✓ | | | ✓ | | | |
| Language teacher | | | ✓ | | | | | ✓ |
| Lawyer | | | ✓ | ✓ | | | | ✓ |
| Legal executive | ✓ | | ✓ | | | | ✓ | ✓ |
| Leisure centre staff | | | | | | | | |

| | V | N | Ve | S | Sp | 3D | Sy | Vo |
|---|---|---|---|---|---|---|---|---|
| Liberal studies teacher | ✓ | | | | | | | |
| Librarian | ✓ | | | | | | ✓ | ✓ |
| Library assistant | | | | | | | ✓ | ✓ |
| Lighthouse keeper | | | | | | | | |
| Lighting technician | | | | | | ✓ | | |
| Linguist | | | ✓ | | | | | ✓ |
| Literary agent | | | ✓ | | | | | ✓ |
| Literary critic | | | ✓ | | | | | ✓ |
| Lock keeper | | | | | | | | |
| Locksmith | | | | | | ✓ | | |
| Locomotive engineer | | ✓ | | | | ✓ | | |
| Lorry driver | | | | | | | | |
| | | | | | | | | |
| Machinist | | | | | | | | |
| Maintenance technician | | | | | | ✓ | | |
| Maître d' | | | | | | | | |
| Make-up artist | | | | | ✓ | | | |
| Management consultant | | ✓ | | ✓ | | | | |
| Managing director | | ✓ | ✓ | ✓ | | | | |
| Marine biologist | ✓ | | | | | | | |
| Market gardener | | | | | | | | |
| Market researcher | | ✓ | | | | | ✓ | |
| Marketing manager | | ✓ | | | ✓ | | | ✓ |
| Masseur/masseuse | | | | | ✓ | | | |
| Materials scientist | | ✓ | | | ✓ | ✓ | | |
| Mathematician | | ✓ | | | ✓ | | | |
| Mechanic | | | | | | ✓ | | |
| Mechanical engineer | | ✓ | | | | ✓ | | |
| Medical illustrator | | | | | ✓ | | | |
| Medical records officer | | | | | | | ✓ | |
| Medical representative | ✓ | | | | | | | |
| Medical secretary | | | | | | | ✓ | |
| Mental nurse | ✓ | | | | | | | |
| Merchandiser | | ✓ | | | | | | |
| Merchant seaman | | | | | | | | |
| Metallurgist | | ✓ | | | | ✓ | | |
| Meteorologist | | | | | ✓ | | | |

**Test Yourself!**

| | V | N | Ve | S | Sp | 3D | Sy | Vo |
|---|---|---|---|---|---|---|---|---|
| Microbiologist | ✔ | ✔ | | | | | | |
| Midwife | ✔ | | | | | | | |
| Milkman | | | | | | | | |
| Miller | | | | | | | | |
| Milliner | | | | | ✔ | | | |
| Miner | | | | | | | | |
| Minister of religion | | | | | | | | ✔ |
| Model (fashion) | | | | | | | | |
| Model maker | | | | | ✔ | ✔ | | |
| Museum assistant | | | | | | | | |
| Music producer | | | | | | | | |
| Music therapist | | | | | | | | |
| Musician | | | | | | | | |
| | | | | | | | | |
| Nanny | | | | | | | | |
| Nature conservancy warden | | | | | | | | |
| Navigating officer | ✔ | ✔ | | | ✔ | | ✔ | |
| Negotiator | | | | | | | | |
| Neurosurgeon | ✔ | ✔ | | ✔ | ✔ | ✔ | | |
| Notary public | | | ✔ | | | | ✔ | ✔ |
| Novelist | | | ✔ | | | | | ✔ |
| Nuclear physicist | ✔ | ✔ | | | ✔ | ✔ | | |
| Nurse | ✔ | | | | | | | |
| Nursery nurse | | | | | | | | |
| Nutritionist | ✔ | | | | | | | |
| | | | | | | | | |
| Obstetrician | ✔ | ✔ | | | ✔ | | | |
| Occupational psychologist | ✔ | ✔ | ✔ | | | | | |
| Occupational therapist | | | | | ✔ | ✔ | | |
| Office cleaner | | | | | | | | |
| Office machinery mechanic | | | | | | ✔ | | |
| Office manager | | ✔ | | | | | ✔ | ✔ |
| Oil rig worker | | | | | | ✔ | | |
| Operational researcher | ✔ | ✔ | | ✔ | ✔ | | ✔ | |
| Ophthalmic optician | ✔ | | | | | ✔ | | |
| Optician (dispensing) | ✔ | | | | | ✔ | ✔ | |
| Organization and methods officer | ✔ | | | ✔ | ✔ | | | |

| | V | N | Ve | S | Sp | 3D | Sy | Vo |
|---|---|---|---|---|---|---|---|---|
| Orthodontist | ✓ | | | | ✓ | ✓ | | |
| Orthoptist | ✓ | | | | ✓ | ✓ | | |
| Osteopath | | | | | ✓ | | | |
| Outplacement consultant | ✓ | | | | | | | ✓ |
| Panel beater | | | | | | ✓ | | |
| Paramedic | ✓ | | | | | | | |
| Patent agent | ✓ | ✓ | ✓ | | ✓ | ✓ | ✓ | ✓ |
| Patent examiner | ✓ | ✓ | ✓ | | ✓ | ✓ | ✓ | ✓ |
| Pathologist | ✓ | ✓ | | | | | | |
| Pattern cutter | | | | | | ✓ | | |
| Personal trainer | | | | | | | | |
| Pharmacist | ✓ | | | | | | ✓ | |
| Pharmacologist | ✓ | | | | ✓ | ✓ | | |
| Philosopher | | | ✓ | ✓ | | | | ✓ |
| Photographer | | | | | ✓ | | | |
| Photographic technician | ✓ | | | | ✓ | | | |
| Physical education teacher | ✓ | | | | | | | |
| Physicist | | ✓ | | | ✓ | ✓ | | |
| Physiotherapist | ✓ | | | | ✓ | | | |
| Piano teacher | | | | | | | | |
| Piano tuner | | | | | | | | |
| Picture framer | | | | | | ✓ | | |
| Pilot (airplane) | | ✓ | | | ✓ | ✓ | | |
| Pilot (coastal) | | | | | ✓ | ✓ | | |
| Plasterer | | ✓ | | | ✓ | | | |
| Play leader | | | | | | | | |
| Plumber | | | | | | ✓ | | |
| Poet | | | ✓ | | | | | ✓ |
| Police dog handler | | | | | | | | |
| Police officer | | | | ✓ | | ✓ | | |
| Political agent | | | | | | | ✓ | ✓ |
| Politician | | | ✓ | | | | | |
| Pool and spa operator | | | | | | | | |
| Post office clerk | | | | | | | ✓ | |
| Poster designer | | | | | ✓ | ✓ | | |
| Postman/woman | | | | | | | | |

| | V | N | Ve | S | Sp | 3D | Sy | Vo |
|---|---|---|---|---|---|---|---|---|
| Potter | | | | | ✓ | | | |
| Press agent | | | ✓ | | | | | |
| Principal nursing officer | ✓ | | | | | | | |
| Printer | | | | | | ✓ | | ✓ |
| Prison officer | | | | | | | | |
| Probation officer | | | | | | | | |
| Producer (films) | | ✓ | | | ✓ | | | ✓ |
| Production manager | | | | | ✓ | | | |
| Programmer | | ✓ | | ✓ | ✓ | ✓ | ✓ | |
| Property negotiator | | | | | | | | |
| Prosthetics engineer | | ✓ | | | | ✓ | | |
| Psychiatric social worker | ✓ | | | | | | ✓ | |
| Psychiatrist | ✓ | | ✓ | | | | | ✓ |
| Psychoanalyst | ✓ | | ✓ | | | | | |
| Psychologist | ✓ | ✓ | ✓ | | | | | |
| Psychotherapist | ✓ | | | | | | | |
| Public relations executive | | | ✓ | | | | | |
| Publican | | | | | | | | |
| Publicity agent | | | ✓ | | | | | |
| Publisher | | | ✓ | | | | | ✓ |
| Purchasing manager | | ✓ | | | ✓ | | ✓ | |
| Purser | | ✓ | | | | | ✓ | |
| Quality controller | | ✓ | | | | ✓ | ✓ | |
| Quality inspector | | ✓ | | | | ✓ | ✓ | |
| Quantity surveyor | ✓ | ✓ | | | ✓ | ✓ | ✓ | |
| Racing car driver | | | | | | | | |
| Radiographer | ✓ | | | | | ✓ | | |
| Railway guard | | | | | | | | |
| Rating valuation officer | ✓ | ✓ | | | | | ✓ | |
| Receptionist | | | | | | | | |
| Recording engineer | | ✓ | | | ✓ | | | |
| Reflexologist | ✓ | | | | | | | |
| Remedial teacher | | | | | | | | |
| Renovator | | | | | ✓ | | | |
| Reporter | | | ✓ | | | | | ✓ |

| | V | N | Ve | S | Sp | 3D | Sy | Vo |
|---|---|---|---|---|---|---|---|---|
| Restorer | | | | | ✓ | | | |
| Retail assistant | | | | | | | | |
| Retail manager | | | | | | | | |
| Roofer | | | | | | ✓ | | |
| Saddler | | | | | ✓ | | | |
| Sailor | | | | | | | | |
| Sales executive | | | | | | | | |
| Sales manager | | ✓ | | ✓ | | | ✓ | ✓ |
| Sales trainer | | | ✓ | ✓ | | | | |
| Salesperson | | | | | | | | |
| Science teacher | ✓ | ✓ | | | | | | |
| Science writer | ✓ | ✓ | | | | | | ✓ |
| Scientific instrument maker | ✓ | | | | | ✓ | | |
| Scriptwriter | | | ✓ | | | | | ✓ |
| Sculptor | | | | | ✓ | | | |
| Secretary/PA | | | | | | | ✓ | |
| Securities analyst | | ✓ | | | | | ✓ | |
| Security officer | | | | | | | | |
| Session musician | | | | | | | | |
| Set designer | | | | | ✓ | ✓ | | |
| Shepherd | | | | | | | | |
| Shipping and forwarding officer | ✓ | | | | | | ✓ | |
| Shop fitter | | | | | | ✓ | | |
| Sign writer | | | | | ✓ | | | |
| Silversmith | | | | | ✓ | | | |
| Social scientist | ✓ | | | | | | | |
| Social worker | | | | | | | | |
| Soldier | | | | | | | | |
| Solicitor | | | ✓ | | | | ✓ | ✓ |
| Sound engineer | | ✓ | | | | ✓ | | |
| Space salesperson | | | | | | | | |
| Speech therapist | ✓ | | | | | | | |
| Sports coach | | | | | | | | |
| Sports official (referee) | | | | | | | | |
| Stage hand | | | | | | | | |
| Stage manager | | | | | ✓ | | | ✓ |

| | V | N | Ve | S | Sp | 3D | Sy | Vo |
|---|---|---|---|---|---|---|---|---|
| Statistician | | ✔ | | ✔ | | | | |
| Stock controller | | ✔ | | | | | ✔ | |
| Stockbroker | | ✔ | | | | | | |
| Stone mason | | | | | ✔ | | | |
| Studio assistant | | | | | | | | |
| Stunt performer | | | | | | | | |
| Surgeon | ✔ | ✔ | | ✔ | ✔ | ✔ | | |
| Surveyor | | ✔ | | | ✔ | | | |
| Systems analyst | | ✔ | | | ✔ | | ✔ | |
| | | | | | | | | |
| Tailor | | | | | ✔ | | | |
| Tax inspector | | ✔ | ✔ | | | | ✔ | |
| Taxi driver | | | | | ✔ | | | |
| Taxidermist | | | | | ✔ | | | |
| Teacher | ✔ | ✔ | ✔ | | | | | |
| Teacher of art/craft | | | | | ✔ | ✔ | | |
| Teacher of handicapped | | | | | | | | |
| Technical illustrator | | | | | ✔ | ✔ | | |
| Technical representative | | | | | ✔ | | | |
| Technical writer | | | | | ✔ | | | ✔ |
| Telecommunications engineer | | ✔ | | | ✔ | | | |
| Telephonist | | | | | | | | |
| Television engineer | | | | | ✔ | | | |
| Television production assistant | | | | | | | | ✔ |
| Thatcher | | | | | ✔ | | | |
| Theatre administrator | ✔ | ✔ | | | | | ✔ | |
| Tiler | | | | | ✔ | | | |
| Tool maker | | | | | ✔ | ✔ | | |
| Toy maker | | | | | ✔ | | | |
| Tracer | | | | | ✔ | ✔ | | |
| Traffic warden | | | | | | | | |
| Train driver | | | | | | | | |
| Training officer | | | ✔ | | | | ✔ | |
| Translator | | ✔ | | | | | ✔ | |
| Transport manager | | | | | | | | |
| Travel agent | | | | | | | ✔ | |

|  | V | N | Ve | S | Sp | 3D | Sy | Vo |
|---|---|---|---|---|---|---|---|---|
| Truck driver |  |  |  |  |  |  |  |  |
| Turf accountant |  | ✔ |  |  |  |  |  |  |
| Umpire |  |  |  |  |  |  |  |  |
| Underwriter |  | ✔ |  |  |  |  | ✔ |  |
| Union negotiator |  |  |  |  |  |  |  |  |
| Upholsterer |  |  |  |  | ✔ |  |  |  |
| Urban planner | ✔ |  |  |  |  | ✔ | ✔ |  |
| Veterinary nurse |  |  |  |  |  |  |  |  |
| Veterinary surgeon | ✔ | ✔ |  |  | ✔ | ✔ |  |  |
| Vision mixer |  |  |  |  |  | ✔ |  |  |
| Vocational counsellor |  |  |  | ✔ |  |  |  | ✔ |
| Waiter/waitress |  |  |  |  |  |  |  |  |
| Watch repairer |  |  |  |  |  | ✔ |  |  |
| Welder |  |  |  |  |  | ✔ |  |  |
| Window dresser |  |  |  |  | ✔ |  |  |  |
| Word processor operator |  |  |  |  |  |  | ✔ |  |
| Work study officer | ✔ |  |  | ✔ |  |  | ✔ |  |
| Writer |  |  | ✔ |  |  |  |  | ✔ |
| Youth worker |  |  |  |  |  |  |  |  |
| Zoo keeper |  |  |  |  | ✔ |  |  |  |
| Zoologist | ✔ | ✔ |  |  |  |  |  |  |

# Part 2

# Personality

# Chapter 10
# Personality test and job satisfaction

## Personality test

Look at each statement in turn. You have to assess yourself in relation to each statement on a scale of 1 to 10.

If you gave yourself a score of 1, this would mean that the statement was not true of you at all.

A score of 10 would mean that the statement described you perfectly. A score of 5 or 6 would mean that the statement is sometimes true for you, and sometimes untrue. Therefore, the larger the score you give yourself, the more you think the statement describes you.

You have to respond to each statement.

You are not being tested, so you cannot be right or wrong. Your answers will give a picture of how you usually are and the way you generally think and feel.

Tick the number in each scale that is true for you. For the time being, pay no attention to the letter at the end of each row. The letter is to assist you in scoring your results and how to do this will be explained later when you have completed the test.

1. I prefer to be left alone to get with my work.

| 1 | 2 | 3 | 4 | 5 | 6 | 7 | 8 | 9 | 10 | | **SO** |
|---|---|---|---|---|---|---|---|---|----|--|--------|

2. I make myself known to everybody.

| 1 | 2 | 3 | 4 | 5 | 6 | 7 | 8 | 9 | 10 | | **A** |
|---|---|---|---|---|---|---|---|---|----|--|-------|

3. I always make sure I get my facts correct.

| 1 | 2 | 3 | 4 | 5 | 6 | 7 | 8 | 9 | 10 | | **F** |
|---|---|---|---|---|---|---|---|---|----|--|-------|

4. I can often speak or act without enough thought.

| 1 | 2 | 3 | 4 | 5 | 6 | 7 | 8 | 9 | 10 | | **SP** |
|---|---|---|---|---|---|---|---|---|----|--|--------|

5. I cannot get difficulties out of my mind.

| 1 | 2 | 3 | 4 | 5 | 6 | 7 | 8 | 9 | 10 | | **I** |
|---|---|---|---|---|---|---|---|---|----|--|-------|

6. I take proper time to prepare for things that might be difficult.

| 1 | 2 | 3 | 4 | 5 | 6 | 7 | 8 | 9 | 10 | | **D** |
|---|---|---|---|---|---|---|---|---|----|--|-------|

7. Nobody stops me from speaking if I have something to say.

| 1 | 2 | 3 | 4 | 5 | 6 | 7 | 8 | 9 | 10 | | **A** |
|---|---|---|---|---|---|---|---|---|----|--|-------|

8. I like it best when someone else takes the lead.

| 1 | 2 | 3 | 4 | 5 | 6 | 7 | 8 | 9 | 10 | | **P** |
|---|---|---|---|---|---|---|---|---|----|--|-------|

9. I do not like to do anything too different from my friends.

| 1 | 2 | 3 | 4 | 5 | 6 | 7 | 8 | 9 | 10 | | **G** |
|---|---|---|---|---|---|---|---|---|----|--|-------|

10. I am affected by how people feel.

| 1 | 2 | 3 | 4 | 5 | 6 | 7 | 8 | 9 | 10 | | I |

11. I make sure that what I do is done as well as it possibly can be.

| 1 | 2 | 3 | 4 | 5 | 6 | 7 | 8 | 9 | 10 | | D |

12. I am quick to sense people's difficulties.

| 1 | 2 | 3 | 4 | 5 | 6 | 7 | 8 | 9 | 10 | | I |

13. I like to avoid dealing with feelings if at all possible.

| 1 | 2 | 3 | 4 | 5 | 6 | 7 | 8 | 9 | 10 | | F |

14. I do not react hastily.

| 1 | 2 | 3 | 4 | 5 | 6 | 7 | 8 | 9 | 10 | | D |

15. I am at my best when working alongside others.

| 1 | 2 | 3 | 4 | 5 | 6 | 7 | 8 | 9 | 10 | | G |

16. I do not like going out very much.

| 1 | 2 | 3 | 4 | 5 | 6 | 7 | 8 | 9 | 10 | | P |

17. To have fun and entertainment in my leisure time is important to me.

| 1 | 2 | 3 | 4 | 5 | 6 | 7 | 8 | 9 | 10 | | SP |

18. I pay no attention to the way others are feeling.

| 1 | 2 | 3 | 4 | 5 | 6 | 7 | 8 | 9 | 10 | | **F** |
|---|---|---|---|---|---|---|---|---|----|--|-------|

19. I get bored easily.

| 1 | 2 | 3 | 4 | 5 | 6 | 7 | 8 | 9 | 10 | | **SP** |
|---|---|---|---|---|---|---|---|---|----|--|--------|

20. I am less sensitive than other people.

| 1 | 2 | 3 | 4 | 5 | 6 | 7 | 8 | 9 | 10 | | **F** |
|---|---|---|---|---|---|---|---|---|----|--|-------|

21. It takes a lot to dent my confidence.

| 1 | 2 | 3 | 4 | 5 | 6 | 7 | 8 | 9 | 10 | | **F** |
|---|---|---|---|---|---|---|---|---|----|--|-------|

22. Always doing something new and different appeals to me.

| 1 | 2 | 3 | 4 | 5 | 6 | 7 | 8 | 9 | 10 | | **SP** |
|---|---|---|---|---|---|---|---|---|----|--|--------|

23. A favourite activity of mine is entertaining friends.

| 1 | 2 | 3 | 4 | 5 | 6 | 7 | 8 | 9 | 10 | | **G** |
|---|---|---|---|---|---|---|---|---|----|--|-------|

24. I control any feelings of annoyance.

| 1 | 2 | 3 | 4 | 5 | 6 | 7 | 8 | 9 | 10 | | **P** |
|---|---|---|---|---|---|---|---|---|----|--|-------|

25. I always speak my mind.

| 1 | 2 | 3 | 4 | 5 | 6 | 7 | 8 | 9 | 10 | | **A** |
|---|---|---|---|---|---|---|---|---|----|--|-------|

26. I can lose sleep because I dwell upon past events.

| 1 | 2 | 3 | 4 | 5 | 6 | 7 | 8 | 9 | 10 | | I |
|---|---|---|---|---|---|---|---|---|----|---|---|

27. I do not look for people to be with.

| 1 | 2 | 3 | 4 | 5 | 6 | 7 | 8 | 9 | 10 | | SO |
|---|---|---|---|---|---|---|---|---|----|---|----|

28. I am a contented person.

| 1 | 2 | 3 | 4 | 5 | 6 | 7 | 8 | 9 | 10 | | D |
|---|---|---|---|---|---|---|---|---|----|---|---|

29. I can easily make decisions by myself.

| 1 | 2 | 3 | 4 | 5 | 6 | 7 | 8 | 9 | 10 | | SO |
|---|---|---|---|---|---|---|---|---|----|---|----|

30. I do not like to persuade people to change their minds.

| 1 | 2 | 3 | 4 | 5 | 6 | 7 | 8 | 9 | 10 | | P |
|---|---|---|---|---|---|---|---|---|----|---|---|

31. I do not find it difficult to stick at one thing.

| 1 | 2 | 3 | 4 | 5 | 6 | 7 | 8 | 9 | 10 | | D |
|---|---|---|---|---|---|---|---|---|----|---|---|

32. I can change my mind at a moment's notice.

| 1 | 2 | 3 | 4 | 5 | 6 | 7 | 8 | 9 | 10 | | SP |
|---|---|---|---|---|---|---|---|---|----|---|----|

33. I am often the one who gets people involved when they get together.

| 1 | 2 | 3 | 4 | 5 | 6 | 7 | 8 | 9 | 10 | | A |
|---|---|---|---|---|---|---|---|---|----|---|---|

34. I see no harm in passing on confidences to my friends.

| 1 | 2 | 3 | 4 | 5 | 6 | 7 | 8 | 9 | 10 | | G |

35. People would consider me insightful.

| 1 | 2 | 3 | 4 | 5 | 6 | 7 | 8 | 9 | 10 | | I |

36. I generally agree if someone feels very strongly about something.

| 1 | 2 | 3 | 4 | 5 | 6 | 7 | 8 | 9 | 10 | | P |

37. I generally win arguments.

| 1 | 2 | 3 | 4 | 5 | 6 | 7 | 8 | 9 | 10 | | A |

38. Having friends is not particularly important to me.

| 1 | 2 | 3 | 4 | 5 | 6 | 7 | 8 | 9 | 10 | | SO |

39. I do not like people to intrude on my space.

| 1 | 2 | 3 | 4 | 5 | 6 | 7 | 8 | 9 | 10 | | SO |

40. I like people to call me anytime.

| 1 | 2 | 3 | 4 | 5 | 6 | 7 | 8 | 9 | 10 | | G |

## Marking the questionnaire

1. Count up your score for each row marked 'SO'. Do the same for 'G' and for the other letters. Place each total in the score chart below. The example shows you how to do this. The maximum you can have for each letter is 50.
2. With each pair of scores, write in the letter or letters associated with the higher score. This is the dominant letter and is written in the chart on the right-hand side in the place provided.

The scores go together in pairs as follows:

| SO and G |
|---|
| A and P |
| I and F |
| SP and D |

3. The difference between the two scores in each pair should be written in to the extreme right section of the score chart.

## Example

| Total Scores | | Dominant Letter | Score Difference |
|---|---|---|---|
| SO = 25 | G = 10 | SO | 15 |
| A = 18 | P = 40 | P | 22 |
| I = 6 | F = 42 | F | 36 |
| SP = 30 | D = 8 | SP | 22 |

Write your own scores in the chart below.

## Score chart

| Total<br>Scores | | Dominant<br>Letter | Score<br>Difference |
|---|---|---|---|
| SO = ..... | G = ..... | ..... | .... |
| A = ..... | P = ..... | ..... | ..... |
| I = ..... | F = ..... | ..... | ..... |
| SP = ..... | D = ..... | ..... | ..... |

# Personality chart

You can place your scores in the chart of personality. You mark your score with a cross (X) at the appropriate place. Scoring is from the centre of the graph. Enter your own score on the left or the right of the graph according to your dominant letter. The example below shows you how.

## Example

| | | | | | |
|---|---|---|---|---|---|
| SO | Solitary | 50454035302520 **X** 10 | 10 1520 253035404550 | G | Gregarious |
| A | Assertive | 50454035302520 15 10 | 10 15**X**253035404550 | P | Passive |
| I | Imaginative | 50454035302520 15 10 | 10 1520 2530**X**404550 | F | Factual |
| SP | Spontaneous | 504540353025**X** 15 10 | 10 1520 253035404550 | D | Deliberate |

The personality characteristics drawn from the example chart are **SO**, **P**, **F** and **SP**, because these are the dominant letters shown by the score differences.

## If your score is borderline

The higher you score for any of the dominant letters, the more noticeably your behaviour will correspond to the description. If your score is borderline, your behaviour may change along that dimension, but may rarely become extremely noticeable. However, you will probably consider that your behaviour is generally more towards one side than the other. Therefore, choose the letter or letters that usually describe your behaviour.

## Personality chart

| | | | | | |
|----|----|----|----|----|----|
| SO | Solitary | 50454035302520 15 10 | 10 1520 253035404550 | G | Gregarious |
| A | Assertive | 50454035302520 15 10 | 10 1520 253035404550 | P | Passive |
| I | Imaginative | 50454035302520 15 10 | 10 1520 253035404550 | F | Factual |
| SP | Spontaneous | 50454035302520 15 10 | 10 1520 253035404550 | D | Deliberate |

Write in your dominant letters here:

# Understanding your personality further

Ask your partner, a friend or colleague to complete the questionnaire for how they perceive you. If the results differ from your own, it could lead to an interesting discussion. It is not that they, or you, are necessarily right or wrong.

In the end, it is up to you which of the results you decide to adopt as the truer representation of yourself. However, where there are differences, it is always enlightening to ask: 1) how different perceptions of you might arise; and also 2) how important these differences might be in career terms.

Although you behave in different ways, depending upon the circumstances you are in or the people you are with, you nevertheless have a personality that remains identifiable. If this were not true, people would not be able to anticipate your reactions; the very fact that there are aspects of you that are predictable testifies to your personality.

This is not to say that your personality will never change. It may well do so, especially if you make efforts to become aware of your potential and give yourself experiences that develop you. However, it seems practical to take your personality as it is now in order to see how it may relate more successfully to one career rather than another.

Different careers do, by and large, require different characteristics. If you work at something that 'suits you' then you will avoid frustration, while your continuing satisfaction and enjoyment are more likely to be assured. It is also true that most careers can be done equally enjoyably by people with widely varying characteristics. It is bound to be so, since no two people are ever completely alike. However, in very broad terms, it makes sense to ask, 'In this career, how would my personality fit?' and, 'Would I enjoy and be successful in this career for the very reason that my personality might be unusual?'

Personality is a complex subject. The aim here is to assist you to assess yourself in relation to some dimensions of personality that are useful in planning your career – what it is about the way you feel and behave that might make you more suited to one career rather than another. To do this, it is best to be honest with yourself as to how you see yourself. There are no rights or wrongs to a test of personality. What is wanted is a description of the real 'you'. Now, just in case you 'undersell' or 'oversell' yourself, you could ask other people who are close to you and know you well to complete the test for the way they see you. If that means you have to photocopy the test it is all right for you to do so for this purpose. Then compare your own responses with that of others.

The most accurate description of 'you' is likely to be the person you are now, the way you behave and the person other people know and recognize. It is possible to answer the test on the basis of assuming how you think you want to be one day, but as you have not got there yet, you will need to think carefully what you have to do to change.

Another factor to consider is whether you might be using only some parts of your personality now, but want to use other parts later on as you develop in your career. For example, if you are factual you might enjoy studying for a scientific career, but later on, if you find yourself working at a laboratory bench, you may find it has too little scope for you if your personality is also gregarious.

## Interpretation of your scores

### People dimensions

The personality test has two dimensions that describe the way you relate to people: 1) whether you tend to be solitary or gregarious; and 2) whether you tend to be assertive or passive:

| **SO – SOLITARY** | **G – GREGARIOUS** |
| --- | --- |
| Self-reliant. Takes initiative on his or her own. Shows initiative. May be seen as either quiet or arrogant. 'Outsider' as an extreme. Works in own way. Can socialize but sometimes shy. Not at ease socially. Detached | Fits in, not necessarily the leader. Seeks company. Hates to be alone. Loyal and provides support. May be easily persuaded by the group out of need to be accepted. Changes behaviour to fit in. Resolves differences |

and purposeful. Makes up own mind. Resourceful. Does not make 'small talk'.

archaeologist, farmworker, chiropodist, interpreter, delivery person, shepherd, silversmith, train driver, writer, craftsperson, photographer, taxi driver, programmer

between others. Participative, enjoys making decisions with others.

airline cabin staff, auctioneer, club secretary, entertainments officer, house parent, play leader, publican, sailor, soldier, youth worker, trainer

## A - ASSERTIVE

Aggressive. May be dominant and stubborn. Seen as 'pushy'. May talk loudly. Gets the point across. Determined, sometimes risk taking, gets what he or she wants. Can 'tread on toes'. May be seen as a 'show off' but also gains respect. May lose sight of how people are affected. Critical. Demanding. Takes responsibility.

broker, club manager, actor, courier, news editor, sales agent, hotel manager, fashion buyer, negotiator, drama teacher, transport manager, reporter

## P - PASSIVE

Keeps matters to himself/herself. Gives way rather than argue. Easy to get on with. Often good team member. Accommodating and not easily annoyed. May avoid saying what is on his or her mind. Avoids confrontation. Tries hard to please. Cooperative, respectful and helpful.

bookbinder, computer operator, dressmaker, engraver, gamekeeper, dietician, gardener, potter, store keeper, technical writer, patent examiner

## Task dimensions

The questionnaire also has two factors that relate to the task: 1) whether you tend to be imaginative or factual; 2) whether you tend to be spontaneous or deliberate:

### I – IMAGINATIVE

Sensitive and aware of people's feelings. Emotional and often expressive. Makes decisions with heart rather than head. Easily affected, hurt by criticism. Spends too much time on small things. Often discouraged and frustrated, but also intuitive and creative. Responsive to feelings and/or ideas.

artist, author (non-technical), musician, dancer, florist, music therapist, speech and drama teacher, window dresser

### F – FACTUAL

Sees things logically. Usually composed and has 'feet on the ground'. Likes orderly, structured behaviour. Not easily distracted, does things in a controlled way. Objective and analytical, sees the essential point. May miss subtle issues that bother others. Likes information and facts.

barrister, camera person, customs officer, diver, estate agent, mechanic, prison officer, technician, traffic warden

### SP – SPONTANEOUS

Lively and impulsive. Likes change and situations which are fast moving and different. Often finds it difficult to stick to one thing or to finish what he or she has started. Amusing and enthusiastic, his or her

### D – DELIBERATE

Calm, stable and dependable. Patient in waiting for things to take their time. Composed and unflustered by events. Takes things as they come. The slow, deliberate approach allows people to depend excitement can infect others. May be seen as lacking 'depth' as he or she chases from one thing to the next. Organization could be forgotten, though he or she might produce a great effect.

upon him or her. Could appear dull or unresponsive. Predictable. Smug – the type who says, 'I told you so.' Copes with pressure. Gets things done in an orderly way.

dancer, demonstrator, dresser, hairdresser, advertising assistant, masseur/masseuse, model, public relations assistant, retail assistant, barperson

ambulance crew, administrator, therapist, draughtsperson, ergonomist, firefighter, security officer, osteopath, restorer, surgeon, work study officer

Your orientation towards the task and the manner in which you relate to people have implications for all careers. Not all of the descriptions will necessarily match you exactly, though the general description they give may be important in relation to different areas of work.

# Description of personality titles

The personality test provides 16 combinations, based upon the eight descriptions that are formed from the four dimensions. For example, a researcher, is solitary, passive, factual and deliberate.

From your own four sets of letters, you can locate yourself in the chart of individual personality titles.

Look first at the top line. Locate yourself to the left or the right of the chart, simply by saying, 'Am I factual or imaginative?'

Then, looking at the bottom line of the chart, ask yourself, 'Am I deliberate or spontaneous?' This will locate you in one of the four columns.

You repeat the procedure by looking at the rows. Looking at the left-hand side of the chart, ask yourself, 'Am I gregarious or solitary?' Then from the right-hand side of the chart, 'Am I assertive or passive?' You will now have located yourself in one of the 16 boxes.

Remember that you are more clearly in one area than another if your scores are more at the extreme end of each dimension. Where your scores are around the middle range, you may consider that, on balance, an adjacent area might be more like you. For example, in the chart below, number 13, a researcher, might be number 9, an arranger, if he or she is a little more assertive.

## Chart of individual personality titles

| TASK | Factual | Factual | Imaginative | Imaginative | PEOPLE |
|------|---------|---------|-------------|-------------|--------|
| Gregarious | 1.<br>Director | 2.<br>Opportunist | 3.<br>Coach | 4.<br>Crusader | Assertive |
| Gregarious | 5.<br>Completer | 6.<br>Associate | 7.<br>Confidant | 8.<br>Colleague | Passive |
| Solitary | 9.<br>Arranger | 10.<br>Adviser | 11.<br>Designer | 12.<br>Idealist | Assertive |
| Solitary | 13.<br>Researcher | 14.<br>Implementer | 15.<br>Specialist | 16.<br>Wanderer | Passive |
| PEOPLE | Deliberate | Spontaneous | Deliberate | Spontaneous | Task |

My dominant letters, from the personality chart, were:

### 1. FDAG – Director
*Characteristics:* Factual, Deliberate, Gregarious and Assertive
*Careers:* armed forces officer, bank manager, general manager, hotel manager, production manager, retail manager, transport manager

### 2. FSpAG – Opportunist
*Characteristics:* Factual, Spontaneous, Assertive and Gregarious
*Careers:* advertising executive, auctioneer, club secretary, estate agent, public relations director, politician, sports coach or manager, senior administrator, funds organizer

### 3. IDAG – Coach
*Characteristics:* Imaginative, Deliberate, Assertive and Gregarious
*Careers:* doctor, osteopath, psychologist, senior nursing officer, senior teacher, social worker, youth worker

### 4. ISpAG – Crusader
*Characteristics:* Independent, Spontaneous, Assertive and Gregarious
*Careers:* civil rights worker, courier, beautician, demonstrator, journalist, public relations executive, drama teacher, union representative

### 5. FDPG – Completer
*Characteristics:* Factual, Deliberate, Passive and Gregarious
*Careers:* ambulance crew, armed forces, cashier, nurse, police officer, prison officer, firefighter, guard

### 6. FSpPG – Associate

*Characteristics:* Factual, Spontaneous, Passive and Gregarious
*Careers:* air hostess or steward, bar person, dental assistant, hairdresser, play leader, junior teacher, secretary, sports or gym assistant, team leader

### 7. IDPG – Confidant

*Characteristics:* Independent, Deliberate, Passive and Gregarious
*Careers:* hospital porter, house parent, mental nurse, nursery teacher, remedial teacher, social worker, therapist

### 8. ISpPG – Colleague

*Characteristics:* Independent, Spontaneous, Passive and Gregarious
*Careers:* counsellor, marketing assistant, nursery nurse, receptionist, retail assistant, stage hand, waiter/waitress

### 9. FDASo – Arranger

*Characteristics:* Factual, Deliberate, Assertive and Solitary
*Careers:* barrister, police inspector, solicitor, work study officer, customs officer, tax inspector

### 10. FSpASo – Adviser

*Characteristics:* Factual, Spontaneous, Assertive and Solitary
*Careers:* importer/exporter, buyer, entrepreneur, commodities or futures broker, sales director, market trader, property speculator, road manager, club manager

### 11. IDASo – Designer

*Characteristics:* Imaginative, Deliberate, Assertive and Solitary
*Careers:* analyst, architect, business consultant, inspector, journalist, librarian, social scientist, medical scientist

## 12. ISpASo – Idealist

*Characteristics:* Independent, Spontaneous, Assertive and Solitary
*Careers:* architect, artist, author, chef, dancer, interior designer, musician, sculptor

## 13. FDPSo – Researcher

*Characteristics:* Factual, Deliberate, Passive and Solitary
*Careers:* accounting technician, actuary, archivist, auditor, driver, engineer, reinsurer, operations researcher

## 14. FSpPSo – Implementer

*Characteristics:* Factual, Spontaneous, Passive and Solitary
*Careers:* accounting technician, tour guide, cook, dietician, interpreter, computer technician, paramedic, road patrol officer, surgeon

## 15. IDPSo – Specialist

*Characteristics:* Independent, Deliberate, Passive and Solitary
*Careers:* arborist, curator, farm worker, site worker, gardener, historian, delivery person, potter, shepherd, thatcher, saddler, gun-maker, planner

## 16. ISpPSo – Wanderer

*Characteristic:* Independent, Spontaneous, Passive and Solitary
*Careers:* bar person, dancer, disc jockey, entertainer, model, porter, production worker, shop assistant, waiter/waitress

# Personality and career profiles

Code
F      Factual
I      Imaginative
S      Spontaneous
D      Deliberate
A      Assertive
P      Passive
G      Group
So      Solitary

| | F | I | S | D | A | P | G | So |
|---|---|---|---|---|---|---|---|---|
| Accident assessor | ✔ | | | ✔ | | | | |
| Accountant | ✔ | | | ✔ | ✔ | | | |
| Accounting technician | ✔ | | | ✔ | | ✔ | | |
| Actor | | ✔ | ✔ | | | | | |
| Actuary | ✔ | | | ✔ | | | | |
| Acupuncturist | ✔ | | | ✔ | | ✔ | | |
| Administrator | ✔ | | | ✔ | | | | |
| Advertising copywriter | | ✔ | | | | | | |
| Advertising executive | | | | | ✔ | | ✔ | |
| Aerobics instructor | | | ✔ | | ✔ | | ✔ | |
| Aeronautical engineer | ✔ | | | ✔ | | | | |
| Aeronautical technician | ✔ | | | ✔ | | ✔ | | |
| Agricultural mechanic | ✔ | | | ✔ | | ✔ | | |
| Agricultural secretary | | | | | | ✔ | | |
| Agriculturalist | ✔ | | | ✔ | | | | |
| Air hostess | | ✔ | ✔ | | | ✔ | ✔ | |
| Air traffic controller | ✔ | | | ✔ | | ✔ | | ✔ |
| Ambulance crew | ✔ | | | ✔ | | ✔ | | |
| Anaesthetist | ✔ | | | ✔ | | ✔ | | ✔ |
| Animal keeper | | | | | | ✔ | | ✔ |
| Animal nurse | ✔ | | | | | ✔ | | ✔ |
| Anthropologist | | | | | | | | ✔ |

**Test Yourself!**

| | F | I | S | D | A | P | G | So |
|---|---|---|---|---|---|---|---|---|
| Antique dealer | | | | | ✓ | | | |
| Appliance repairer | ✓ | | | | | ✓ | | ✓ |
| Arborist | | | | | | ✓ | | ✓ |
| Aromatherapist | | ✓ | ✓ | | | ✓ | ✓ | |
| Architect | | ✓ | | ✓ | ✓ | | | ✓ |
| Architectural technician | | ✓ | | ✓ | | ✓ | | ✓ |
| Archivist | | | | ✓ | | ✓ | | ✓ |
| Armed forces officer | ✓ | | | | | ✓ | ✓ | |
| Armed forces personnel | ✓ | | | | | | ✓ | |
| Art dealer | | ✓ | | ✓ | | | | |
| Art restorer | | ✓ | | ✓ | | ✓ | | ✓ |
| Art therapist | | ✓ | | | | ✓ | | ✓ |
| Artist | | ✓ | | | | | | ✓ |
| Arts adminstrator | ✓ | | | | | | ✓ | |
| Astronaut | ✓ | | | ✓ | | ✓ | | |
| Atronomer | ✓ | | | ✓ | | ✓ | | ✓ |
| Auctioneer | ✓ | | ✓ | | ✓ | | | ✓ |
| Audiology technician | ✓ | | | | | ✓ | | ✓ |
| Auditor | ✓ | | | ✓ | | ✓ | | ✓ |
| Author | | ✓ | | | | | | ✓ |
| Automobile technician | ✓ | | | | | ✓ | | ✓ |
| | | | | | | | | |
| Bacteriologist | ✓ | | | | | ✓ | | ✓ |
| Baggage handler | | | | | | | | ✓ |
| Baker | | | ✓ | | | ✓ | | ✓ |
| Ballet dancer | | ✓ | ✓ | | | ✓ | | |
| Bank clerk | ✓ | | | ✓ | | ✓ | | |
| Bank manager | ✓ | | | ✓ | ✓ | | ✓ | |
| Barperson | | ✓ | ✓ | | | ✓ | ✓ | |
| Barrister | ✓ | | | | ✓ | | | |
| Beautician | | ✓ | ✓ | | | | ✓ | |
| Bicycle repairer | | | | | | ✓ | | ✓ |
| Bilingual secretary | | ✓ | | | | ✓ | | ✓ |
| Biologist | ✓ | | | | | ✓ | | ✓ |
| Biomedical engineer | ✓ | | | ✓ | | ✓ | | ✓ |
| Blacksmith/farrier | | | | | | ✓ | | ✓ |
| Boat builder | | | | | | ✓ | | ✓ |

| | F | I | S | D | A | P | G | So |
|---|---|---|---|---|---|---|---|---|
| Bookbinder | | | | | | ✓ | | ✓ |
| Book critic | | ✓ | ✓ | | | | | ✓ |
| Book illustrator | | ✓ | | | | ✓ | | ✓ |
| Bookseller | | | | ✓ | | | | |
| Botanist | | | ✓ | | | ✓ | | ✓ |
| Brewer | ✓ | | | | | | | |
| Bricklayer | | | ✓ | | | ✓ | | ✓ |
| Broker | ✓ | | ✓ | | ✓ | | | |
| Builder's merchant | ✓ | | | | | | | |
| Building demolition expert | | | ✓ | | | ✓ | | ✓ |
| Building inspector | ✓ | | ✓ | | | ✓ | | ✓ |
| Building society assistant | ✓ | | ✓ | | | ✓ | | |
| Building society manager | ✓ | | ✓ | | | | ✓ | |
| Building surveyor | ✓ | | ✓ | | | ✓ | | ✓ |
| Bursar | ✓ | | ✓ | | | ✓ | | |
| Bus driver | | | | | | ✓ | | ✓ |
| Business consultant | ✓ | | | | ✓ | | | |
| Buyer | | ✓ | | ✓ | ✓ | | | |
| | | | | | | | | |
| Cabinet maker | | ✓ | | ✓ | | ✓ | | ✓ |
| Camera repairer | | ✓ | | | | ✓ | | ✓ |
| Car body designer | | ✓ | ✓ | | | | | |
| Careers adviser | | | | ✓ | | | | |
| Carpenter | | ✓ | | | | ✓ | | ✓ |
| Cartographer | | | ✓ | | | ✓ | | ✓ |
| Cartoon animator | | ✓ | ✓ | | | ✓ | | ✓ |
| Cashier | ✓ | | ✓ | | | ✓ | | |
| Caterer | | ✓ | | ✓ | | | ✓ | |
| CD-ROM producer | | ✓ | | ✓ | ✓ | | | |
| Chef | | ✓ | ✓ | ✓ | | | | ✓ |
| Chemical technician | ✓ | | ✓ | | | ✓ | | ✓ |
| Chemical technologist | ✓ | | ✓ | | | ✓ | | ✓ |
| Chemist | ✓ | | ✓ | | | | | ✓ |
| Chief executive | | | | ✓ | | | | |
| Child care worker | | | | | | ✓ | ✓ | |
| Chimney sweep | | | ✓ | | | ✓ | | ✓ |
| Chiropodist | | | ✓ | | | ✓ | | ✓ |

**Test Yourself!**

| | F | I | S | D | A | P | G | So |
|---|---|---|---|---|---|---|---|---|
| Choreographer | | ✔ | ✔ | | | | | |
| Cinema manager | | ✔ | | ✔ | ✔ | ✔ | | |
| Civil engineer | ✔ | | ✔ | | | | | |
| Civil servant | | ✔ | ✔ | | | | | |
| Clerk | ✔ | | ✔ | | | ✔ | | |
| Clinical psychologist | ✔ | | | | | ✔ | | |
| Clown | | ✔ | ✔ | | | ✔ | | |
| Club manager | | ✔ | | | ✔ | ✔ | | |
| Coastguard | | | | ✔ | | ✔ | | |
| College admissions counsellor | | | | | | ✔ | | |
| Comic illustrator | ✔ | | | | | | | ✔ |
| Commercial account manager | ✔ | | | | ✔ | | | |
| Community social worker | ✔ | | | | | ✔ | ✔ | |
| Community warden | | | | | | ✔ | ✔ | |
| Company secretary | ✔ | | ✔ | | | ✔ | | ✔ |
| Compositor | | ✔ | ✔ | | | ✔ | | ✔ |
| Computer animator | | ✔ | ✔ | | | | | |
| Computer game designer | | ✔ | ✔ | | | ✔ | | ✔ |
| Computer hardware designer | ✔ | | ✔ | | | | | |
| Computer systems analyst | | | ✔ | | | | | ✔ |
| Computer technician | ✔ | | ✔ | | | ✔ | | ✔ |
| Confectioner | | ✔ | | | | ✔ | | |
| Conference organizer | | | ✔ | ✔ | | ✔ | | |
| Conservation officer | | | ✔ | | | ✔ | | ✔ |
| Copywriter | | ✔ | | | | | | ✔ |
| Coroner | ✔ | | ✔ | | | ✔ | | |
| Cost accountant | ✔ | | ✔ | | | ✔ | | |
| Counsellor | | ✔ | ✔ | | | ✔ | ✔ | |
| Courier | | | ✔ | | | | | ✔ |
| Court reporter | ✔ | | ✔ | | | | | ✔ |
| Crane operator | | | | | | | | ✔ |
| Criminologist | | | ✔ | ✔ | | | | |
| Cruise director | | | | ✔ | | ✔ | | |
| Cryptographer | ✔ | | ✔ | | | ✔ | | ✔ |
| Cultural anthropologist | | | ✔ | | | ✔ | | ✔ |

| | F | I | S | D | A | P | G | So |
|---|---|---|---|---|---|---|---|---|
| Curator | | ✓ | ✓ | | | ✓ | | ✓ |
| Currency trader | ✓ | | ✓ | ✓ | | ✓ | | |
| Customer services manager | | | ✓ | | | ✓ | ✓ | |
| Customs officer | ✓ | | | ✓ | ✓ | | | ✓ |
| | | | | | | | | |
| Dance instructor | | ✓ | ✓ | | | ✓ | | |
| Dancer | | ✓ | ✓ | | | | | |
| Deaf interpreter | | | | | | ✓ | | |
| Decorator | | ✓ | | | | | | ✓ |
| Demonstrator | | | ✓ | ✓ | | | | ✓ |
| Dental assistant | ✓ | | | ✓ | ✓ | | | |
| Dental hygienist | ✓ | | | ✓ | ✓ | | | |
| Dental nurse | ✓ | | | ✓ | ✓ | | | |
| Dental technician | ✓ | | | ✓ | ✓ | | | ✓ |
| Dentist | ✓ | | | ✓ | ✓ | | | |
| Dermatologist | ✓ | | | ✓ | ✓ | | | ✓ |
| Design engineer | | ✓ | | ✓ | | | | |
| Designer | | ✓ | ✓ | | | | | ✓ |
| Dietician | ✓ | | | | ✓ | | | ✓ |
| Director (media) | | ✓ | | ✓ | | | ✓ | |
| Disc jockey | | ✓ | ✓ | ✓ | | | | |
| Dispensing optician | ✓ | | | ✓ | ✓ | | | ✓ |
| Display artist | | ✓ | ✓ | | | ✓ | | |
| Diver | ✓ | | | ✓ | ✓ | | | ✓ |
| Doctor of medicine | ✓ | | | ✓ | ✓ | | | |
| Drama teacher | | ✓ | ✓ | ✓ | | | ✓ | |
| Draughtsperson | | | ✓ | ✓ | | | | ✓ |
| Dresser (stage) | | ✓ | ✓ | | | ✓ | | ✓ |
| Dressmaker | | ✓ | ✓ | | | ✓ | | ✓ |
| Driver | | | ✓ | ✓ | | ✓ | | ✓ |
| Drug and alcohol counsellor | | ✓ | | | | ✓ | | |
| Drycleaner | ✓ | | | ✓ | | | | |
| | | | | | | | | |
| Ecologist | | ✓ | | ✓ | ✓ | | | |
| Economist | ✓ | | | ✓ | | | | |
| Editor | | ✓ | | ✓ | ✓ | | | |
| Editor (newspapers) | | ✓ | ✓ | | ✓ | | ✓ | |

| | F | I | S | D | A | P | G | So |
|---|---|---|---|---|---|---|---|---|
| Editorial cartoonist | | ✔ | ✔ | | | ✔ | | |
| Educational psychologist | | | | | | ✔ | | ✔ |
| Electrical engineer | ✔ | | | ✔ | | | | |
| Electrician | ✔ | | | ✔ | | | | ✔ |
| Electronics engineer | ✔ | | | ✔ | | | | ✔ |
| Elementary school teacher | | ✔ | | | | ✔ | | |
| Embalmer | | | | ✔ | | ✔ | | ✔ |
| Employment officer | | | | ✔ | | | | |
| Engineering pattern maker | ✔ | | | ✔ | | ✔ | | ✔ |
| Engineering technician | ✔ | | | ✔ | | | | |
| English language teacher | | ✔ | ✔ | | | ✔ | | |
| Engraver | | ✔ | ✔ | | | ✔ | | ✔ |
| Entertainments officer | | ✔ | ✔ | | | | | |
| Environmental health officer | ✔ | | | ✔ | | | | ✔ |
| Equestrian | | | | | | ✔ | | |
| Ergonomist | ✔ | | | ✔ | | ✔ | | ✔ |
| Estate agent | | | | | ✔ | | ✔ | |
| Estate manager | | | | ✔ | ✔ | | | |
| Exhibition organizer | | ✔ | ✔ | | | ✔ | ✔ | |
| Explosives expert | ✔ | | | ✔ | | | | ✔ |
| Farm manager | ✔ | | | ✔ | ✔ | | | |
| Farmer | | | | | | | | ✔ |
| Farmworker | | | | | | ✔ | | ✔ |
| Fashion buyer | | ✔ | ✔ | ✔ | | | | |
| Fashion designer | | ✔ | ✔ | | | ✔ | | |
| Film projectionist | | ✔ | | | | ✔ | | ✔ |
| Film reviewer | | ✔ | | | | | | ✔ |
| Financial analyst | ✔ | | | ✔ | | ✔ | | ✔ |
| Financial controller | ✔ | | | ✔ | ✔ | | | |
| Firefighter | | | | ✔ | | | | ✔ |
| Fisheries officer | ✔ | | | ✔ | | | | |
| Fisherman | | | | | | | | ✔ |
| Fitter | | | | | | ✔ | | ✔ |
| Flight attendant | | ✔ | | ✔ | | ✔ | ✔ | |
| Florist | | ✔ | ✔ | | | ✔ | | ✔ |
| Flyperson (theatre) | | ✔ | ✔ | | | ✔ | | ✔ |

|                              | F | I | S | D | A | P | G | So |
|------------------------------|---|---|---|---|---|---|---|----|
| Food hygiene inspector       | ✔ |   |   | ✔ |   | ✔ |   |    |
| Food service worker          |   |   |   |   |   |   | ✔ |    |
| Foreign correspondent        |   | ✔ | ✔ |   | ✔ |   |   | ✔  |
| Foreign language teacher     |   | ✔ | ✔ |   |   | ✔ |   |    |
| Forensic pathologist         | ✔ |   |   | ✔ |   | ✔ |   | ✔  |
| Forensic psychologist        | ✔ |   |   | ✔ |   | ✔ |   | ✔  |
| Forensic scientist           | ✔ |   |   | ✔ |   | ✔ |   | ✔  |
| Forester                     |   |   |   |   |   | ✔ |   | ✔  |
| Freelance writer             |   | ✔ | ✔ |   |   | ✔ |   | ✔  |
| Fund raiser                  |   | ✔ |   | ✔ | ✔ |   | ✔ |    |
| Funeral director             | ✔ |   |   | ✔ | ✔ |   |   |    |
| Furniture maker              |   | ✔ |   | ✔ |   | ✔ |   | ✔  |
|                              |   |   |   |   |   |   |   |    |
| Gamekeeper                   |   |   |   |   |   | ✔ | ✔ |    |
| Gardener                     |   |   |   |   |   | ✔ |   | ✔  |
| Genealogist                  | ✔ |   |   | ✔ |   | ✔ |   | ✔  |
| Geneticist                   | ✔ |   |   | ✔ |   |   |   | ✔  |
| Geochemist                   | ✔ |   |   | ✔ |   | ✔ |   | ✔  |
| Geologist                    | ✔ |   |   | ✔ |   | ✔ |   | ✔  |
| Glassblower                  |   |   |   |   |   | ✔ |   | ✔  |
| Glazier                      |   |   |   |   |   | ✔ |   |    |
| Golf professional            |   |   |   |   | ✔ |   | ✔ |    |
| Graphic designer             |   | ✔ | ✔ |   |   | ✔ |   | ✔  |
| Grocer                       |   |   |   | ✔ | ✔ |   |   |    |
| Groundsperson                |   |   |   | ✔ |   | ✔ |   | ✔  |
| Guard                        | ✔ |   |   | ✔ |   |   |   | ✔  |
| Gunsmith                     |   |   |   | ✔ |   | ✔ |   | ✔  |
|                              |   |   |   |   |   |   |   |    |
| Hairdresser                  |   | ✔ | ✔ |   |   |   | ✔ |    |
| Head teacher                 |   |   |   |   | ✔ |   | ✔ |    |
| Health services administrator| ✔ |   |   | ✔ |   |   |   |    |
| Health visitor               | ✔ |   |   | ✔ |   | ✔ |   |    |
| Heating engineer             | ✔ |   |   |   |   |   |   | ✔  |
| Historian                    |   |   |   |   |   | ✔ |   | ✔  |
| Homeopath                    | ✔ |   |   | ✔ |   | ✔ |   |    |
| Horologist                   |   |   |   | ✔ |   | ✔ |   | ✔  |

**Test Yourself!**

| | F | I | S | D | A | P | G | So |
|---|---|---|---|---|---|---|---|---|
| Horticulturalist | | | | | | ✔ | | ✔ |
| Hospital physicist | ✔ | | ✔ | | | ✔ | | |
| Hospital porter | | | | | | ✔ | | |
| Hostel warden | | | | | | | ✔ | |
| **Hotel manager** | | | | ✔ | | | ✔ | |
| House parent | | | | | | ✔ | ✔ | |
| Housing manager | ✔ | | ✔ | | | ✔ | | |
| Human resources manager | | | | | ✔ | | | |
| Hydrographic surveyor | ✔ | | ✔ | | | | | ✔ |
| Hydrologist | ✔ | | ✔ | | | ✔ | | ✔ |
| | | | | | | | | |
| Illustrator | | ✔ | ✔ | | | | | ✔ |
| Immunologist | ✔ | | ✔ | | | ✔ | | |
| Importer/exporter | | | | | ✔ | | | |
| Industrial designer | | ✔ | ✔ | | | | | |
| Industrial nurse | ✔ | | ✔ | | | ✔ | | |
| Industrial relations officer | | | | | ✔ | | | |
| Information officer | | ✔ | | | | ✔ | ✔ | |
| Information scientist | ✔ | | ✔ | | | ✔ | | ✔ |
| Instrument and control engineer | ✔ | | ✔ | | | ✔ | | ✔ |
| Instrument maker | ✔ | | ✔ | | | ✔ | | |
| Insurance adjuster | ✔ | | ✔ | | | | | |
| Insurange agent | ✔ | | ✔ | | ✔ | | | ✔ |
| Interior designer | | ✔ | ✔ | | | | | |
| Interpreter | | ✔ | ✔ | | | ✔ | | ✔ |
| Interviewer | | ✔ | | | ✔ | | | |
| | | | | | | | | |
| Jewellery maker | | ✔ | ✔ | | | ✔ | | ✔ |
| Jockey | | | ✔ | | ✔ | | | |
| Joiner | | | | | | ✔ | | ✔ |
| Journalist | | ✔ | ✔ | | ✔ | | | |
| Judge | | | | ✔ | ✔ | | | ✔ |
| Justices clerk | | | ✔ | | | | | ✔ |
| | | | | | | | | |
| Laboratory technician | ✔ | | ✔ | | | ✔ | | |
| Landscape architect | | ✔ | ✔ | | | | | ✔ |

| | F | I | S | D | A | P | G | So |
|---|---|---|---|---|---|---|---|---|
| Language teacher | | ✔ | ✔ | | | ✔ | | |
| Lawyer | | | | ✔ | ✔ | | | |
| Legal executive | | | | ✔ | | ✔ | | |
| Leisure centre staff | | | ✔ | | | | ✔ | |
| Liberal studies teacher | ✔ | ✔ | | | | | | |
| Librarian | | ✔ | | ✔ | | ✔ | | ✔ |
| Library assistant | | ✔ | | ✔ | | ✔ | | ✔ |
| Lighthouse keeper | | | | | | ✔ | | ✔ |
| Lighting technician | ✔ | | | ✔ | | ✔ | | ✔ |
| Linguist | | ✔ | ✔ | | | ✔ | ✔ | |
| Literary agent | | ✔ | | ✔ | ✔ | | | |
| Literary critic | | ✔ | ✔ | ✔ | | | | |
| Lock keeper | | | | | | ✔ | | ✔ |
| Locksmith | ✔ | | | ✔ | | | | ✔ |
| Locomotive engineer | ✔ | | | ✔ | | ✔ | | ✔ |
| Lorry driver | | | | | | ✔ | | ✔ |
| | | | | | | | | |
| Machinist | | | | | | ✔ | | ✔ |
| Maintenance technician | ✔ | | | ✔ | | ✔ | | |
| Maître d' | | ✔ | ✔ | | ✔ | | ✔ | |
| Make-up artist | | ✔ | ✔ | | | | | |
| Management consultant | ✔ | | ✔ | | | ✔ | ✔ | |
| Managing director | | | | ✔ | ✔ | | ✔ | |
| Marine biologist | ✔ | | | ✔ | | ✔ | | |
| Market gardener | | ✔ | | ✔ | | | | |
| Market researcher | | ✔ | | ✔ | ✔ | | | |
| Marketing manager | | ✔ | | ✔ | ✔ | | | |
| Masseur/masseuse | | ✔ | ✔ | | | ✔ | | |
| Materials scientist | ✔ | | | ✔ | | | | |
| Mathematician | ✔ | | ✔ | | | | | |
| Mechanic | ✔ | | | ✔ | | ✔ | | ✔ |
| Mechanical engineer | ✔ | | | ✔ | | | | |
| Medical illustrator | | ✔ | | ✔ | | ✔ | | ✔ |
| Medical records officer | ✔ | | | ✔ | | | | |
| Medical representative | | | ✔ | | ✔ | | | ✔ |
| Medical secretary | | ✔ | | ✔ | | ✔ | | |
| Mental nurse | | ✔ | | ✔ | | ✔ | ✔ | |

| | F | I | S | D | A | P | G | So |
|---|---|---|---|---|---|---|---|---|
| Merchandiser | | ✔ | ✔ | ✔ | | | | |
| Merchant seaman | ✔ | | ✔ | | | ✔ | | ✔ |
| Metallurgist | ✔ | | ✔ | | | | | |
| Meteorologist | ✔ | | ✔ | | | ✔ | | ✔ |
| Microbiologist | ✔ | | ✔ | | | | | ✔ |
| Midwife | ✔ | | ✔ | ✔ | | | ✔ | |
| Milkman | | ✔ | | | | ✔ | | ✔ |
| Miller | ✔ | | | | | ✔ | | |
| Milliner | | ✔ | ✔ | | | ✔ | | ✔ |
| Miner | | | ✔ | | | ✔ | ✔ | |
| Minister of religion | ✔ | | | ✔ | | | | ✔ |
| Model (fashion) | ✔ | ✔ | | | | | | |
| Model maker | ✔ | | ✔ | | | ✔ | | ✔ |
| Museum assistant | ✔ | | ✔ | | | ✔ | | |
| Music producer | ✔ | | ✔ | ✔ | | | | |
| Music therapist | ✔ | ✔ | | | | ✔ | | |
| Musician | ✔ | ✔ | | | | | | |
| Nanny | ✔ | ✔ | | | | ✔ | | |
| Nature conservancy warden | ✔ | | ✔ | | | | | ✔ |
| Navigating officer | ✔ | | ✔ | | | ✔ | | |
| Negotiator | ✔ | | ✔ | ✔ | | | | |
| Neurosurgeon | ✔ | | ✔ | | | | | |
| Notary public | | | ✔ | | | ✔ | | |
| Novelist | | ✔ | ✔ | | | | | ✔ |
| Nuclear physicist | ✔ | | ✔ | | | | | |
| Nurse | ✔ | | ✔ | | | ✔ | ✔ | |
| Nursery nurse | | ✔ | ✔ | | | ✔ | | |
| Nutritionist | ✔ | | ✔ | | | ✔ | | ✔ |
| Obstetrician | ✔ | | ✔ | | | | | |
| Occupational psychologist | ✔ | | ✔ | ✔ | | | | |
| Occupational therapist | | ✔ | ✔ | | | ✔ | | ✔ |
| Office cleaner | | | ✔ | | | ✔ | | ✔ |
| Office machinery mechanic | | | ✔ | | | ✔ | | ✔ |
| Office manager | ✔ | | ✔ | ✔ | | | | |
| Oil rig worker | ✔ | | ✔ | | | ✔ | | |

|  | F | I | S | D | A | P | G | So |
|---|---|---|---|---|---|---|---|---|
| Operational researcher | ✔ |  | ✔ |  |  |  |  | ✔ |
| Ophthalmic optician | ✔ |  | ✔ |  |  | ✔ |  | ✔ |
| Optician (dispensing) | ✔ | ✔ |  | ✔ |  |  |  |  |
| Organization and methods officer | ✔ |  | ✔ |  |  |  |  |  |
| Orthodontist | ✔ |  | ✔ |  |  | ✔ |  |  |
| Orthoptist | ✔ |  | ✔ |  |  | ✔ |  |  |
| Osteopath |  | ✔ |  | ✔ | ✔ |  |  | ✔ |
| Outplacement consultant |  | ✔ |  | ✔ | ✔ |  | ✔ |  |
| Panel beater |  |  | ✔ |  |  |  |  | ✔ |
| Paramedic | ✔ |  | ✔ |  |  |  |  |  |
| Patent agent | ✔ |  | ✔ | ✔ |  |  |  |  |
| Patent examiner | ✔ |  | ✔ |  |  | ✔ |  | ✔ |
| Pathologist | ✔ |  | ✔ |  |  |  |  |  |
| Pattern cutter |  | ✔ | ✔ |  |  | ✔ |  |  |
| Personal trainer |  |  | ✔ |  | ✔ |  | ✔ |  |
| Pharmacist | ✔ |  | ✔ | ✔ |  |  |  |  |
| Pharmacologist | ✔ |  | ✔ |  |  | ✔ |  | ✔ |
| Philosopher |  | ✔ | ✔ |  |  |  |  | ✔ |
| Photographer |  | ✔ | ✔ |  |  | ✔ |  | ✔ |
| Photographic technician | ✔ |  | ✔ |  |  | ✔ |  | ✔ |
| Physical education teacher | ✔ |  | ✔ | ✔ |  |  | ✔ |  |
| Physicist | ✔ |  | ✔ |  |  | ✔ |  | ✔ |
| Physiotherapist |  | ✔ | ✔ |  |  | ✔ |  | ✔ |
| Piano teacher | ✔ | ✔ |  |  |  | ✔ |  |  |
| Piano tuner |  | ✔ | ✔ |  |  |  |  | ✔ |
| Picture framer |  | ✔ | ✔ |  |  |  |  | ✔ |
| Pilot (airplane) | ✔ |  | ✔ |  |  | ✔ |  | ✔ |
| Pilot (coastal) | ✔ |  | ✔ |  |  |  |  |  |
| Plasterer |  | ✔ | ✔ |  |  |  |  | ✔ |
| Play leader |  | ✔ | ✔ |  |  | ✔ | ✔ |  |
| Plumber | ✔ |  |  |  |  |  |  | ✔ |
| Poet |  | ✔ | ✔ |  |  | ✔ |  | ✔ |
| Police dog handler | ✔ |  |  |  |  |  |  | ✔ |
| Police officer |  |  |  | ✔ | ✔ |  |  |  |
| Political agent |  |  |  |  | ✔ |  | ✔ |  |

# Test Yourself!

| | F | I | S | D | A | P | G | So |
|---|---|---|---|---|---|---|---|---|
| Politician | | ✓ | | | ✓ | ✓ | | |
| Pool and spa operator | ✓ | | | | | | | |
| Poster designer | | ✓ | ✓ | | | ✓ | | ✓ |
| Postman/woman | | | ✓ | | | ✓ | | ✓ |
| Post office clerk | | | | ✓ | | ✓ | | |
| Potter | | ✓ | ✓ | | | ✓ | | ✓ |
| Press agent | | ✓ | ✓ | | ✓ | | ✓ | |
| Principal nursing officer | ✓ | | | ✓ | ✓ | | ✓ | |
| Printer | | ✓ | | ✓ | | ✓ | | ✓ |
| Prison officer | ✓ | | | ✓ | | ✓ | | |
| Probation officer | | | | ✓ | ✓ | | | |
| Producer (films) | | ✓ | | ✓ | ✓ | | ✓ | |
| Production manager | | ✓ | ✓ | ✓ | ✓ | | ✓ | |
| Programmer | ✓ | | | ✓ | ✓ | | | ✓ |
| Property negotiator | ✓ | | ✓ | ✓ | | | | |
| Prosthetics engineer | ✓ | | | ✓ | | ✓ | | ✓ |
| Psychiatric social worker | | ✓ | ✓ | ✓ | | | | ✓ |
| Psychiatrist | | ✓ | | ✓ | | ✓ | | ✓ |
| Psychoanalyst | | ✓ | ✓ | | | ✓ | | ✓ |
| Psychologist | | | | | | ✓ | | ✓ |
| Psychotherapist | | ✓ | ✓ | | | ✓ | | ✓ |
| Public relations executive | | ✓ | | ✓ | ✓ | | ✓ | |
| Publican | ✓ | | ✓ | | ✓ | ✓ | | |
| Publicity agent | | ✓ | ✓ | ✓ | | | ✓ | |
| Publisher | | ✓ | | ✓ | ✓ | | | |
| Purchasing manager | ✓ | | ✓ | ✓ | | | | |
| Purser | ✓ | | | ✓ | | ✓ | | |
| Quality controller | ✓ | | | ✓ | | | | |
| Quality inspector | ✓ | | | ✓ | ✓ | | | ✓ |
| Quantity surveyor | ✓ | | | ✓ | | ✓ | | ✓ |
| Racing car driver | ✓ | | ✓ | ✓ | | | | |
| Radiographer | ✓ | | | ✓ | | ✓ | | ✓ |
| Railway guard | | | | ✓ | ✓ | | | ✓ |
| Rating valuation officer | ✓ | | | ✓ | | | | |
| Receptionist | | ✓ | ✓ | | | ✓ | ✓ | |

# Personality Test and Job Satisfaction

| | F | I | S | D | A | P | G | So |
|---|---|---|---|---|---|---|---|---|
| Recording engineer | ✔ | | ✔ | | | ✔ | | ✔ |
| Reflexologist | | ✔ | ✔ | | | ✔ | | ✔ |
| Remedial teacher | | | ✔ | | | ✔ | | |
| Renovator | | ✔ | ✔ | | | ✔ | | ✔ |
| Reporter | | ✔ | ✔ | | ✔ | | | ✔ |
| Restorer | | ✔ | ✔ | | | ✔ | | ✔ |
| Retail assistant | | | | | | ✔ | ✔ | |
| Retail manager | | | | | ✔ | | ✔ | |
| Roofer | | | ✔ | | | ✔ | | ✔ |
| | | | | | | | | |
| Saddler | | ✔ | | ✔ | | ✔ | | ✔ |
| Sailor | ✔ | | ✔ | | | ✔ | | |
| Sales executive | | | ✔ | ✔ | | | | |
| Sales manager | | | | ✔ | | | ✔ | |
| Sales trainer | | ✔ | ✔ | ✔ | | | | |
| Salesperson | | | ✔ | ✔ | | | | |
| Science teacher | ✔ | | ✔ | | | ✔ | | |
| Science writer | | ✔ | ✔ | | | ✔ | | ✔ |
| Scientific instrument maker | ✔ | | | ✔ | | ✔ | | ✔ |
| Scriptwriter | | ✔ | ✔ | | | | | ✔ |
| Sculptor | | ✔ | ✔ | | ✔ | | | ✔ |
| Secretary/PA | | ✔ | | ✔ | | ✔ | | |
| Securities analyst | ✔ | | | ✔ | | | | ✔ |
| Security officer | ✔ | | | ✔ | | ✔ | | ✔ |
| Session musician | | ✔ | ✔ | | | ✔ | | |
| Set designer | | ✔ | ✔ | | | ✔ | | ✔ |
| Shepherd | | | | ✔ | | ✔ | | ✔ |
| Shipping and forwarding officer | ✔ | | | ✔ | | | | |
| Shop fitter | ✔ | | | | | | | |
| Sign writer | | ✔ | | ✔ | | ✔ | | ✔ |
| Silversmith | | ✔ | | ✔ | | ✔ | | ✔ |
| Social scientist | | ✔ | | | | ✔ | | |
| Social worker | | ✔ | | ✔ | ✔ | | | |
| Soldier | ✔ | | ✔ | | | ✔ | | |
| Solicitor | | ✔ | | ✔ | | ✔ | | |
| Sound engineer | ✔ | | | ✔ | | | | ✔ |

## Test Yourself!

| | F | I | S | D | A | P | G | So |
|---|---|---|---|---|---|---|---|---|
| Space salesperson | | ✔ | ✔ | ✔ | | | | ✔ |
| Speech therapist | | ✔ | ✔ | | | ✔ | | ✔ |
| Sports coach | | | ✔ | | ✔ | | ✔ | |
| Sports official (referee) | | | ✔ | | | ✔ | | ✔ |
| Stage hand | | ✔ | ✔ | | | ✔ | | ✔ |
| Stage manager | | ✔ | ✔ | ✔ | | | | |
| Statistician | ✔ | | | ✔ | | ✔ | | ✔ |
| Stock controller | ✔ | | | ✔ | | ✔ | | ✔ |
| Stockbroker | ✔ | | ✔ | ✔ | | | | |
| Stone mason | | ✔ | ✔ | | | ✔ | | ✔ |
| Studio assistant | | ✔ | ✔ | | | ✔ | | |
| Stunt performer | | ✔ | ✔ | ✔ | | | | ✔ |
| Surgeon | ✔ | | | ✔ | | ✔ | | ✔ |
| Surveyor | ✔ | | | ✔ | | ✔ | | ✔ |
| Systems analyst | ✔ | | ✔ | | | | | |
| Tailor | | ✔ | ✔ | | | | | ✔ |
| Tax inspector | ✔ | | | ✔ | | ✔ | | ✔ |
| Taxi driver | | | | | | ✔ | | ✔ |
| Taxidermist | | ✔ | | ✔ | | | | ✔ |
| Teacher | | | | | | ✔ | ✔ | |
| Teacher of art/craft | | ✔ | ✔ | | | ✔ | | ✔ |
| Teacher of handicapped | | | | | | ✔ | | |
| Technical illustrator | | ✔ | | ✔ | | ✔ | | ✔ |
| Technical representative | ✔ | ✔ | | ✔ | ✔ | | | ✔ |
| Technical writer | | ✔ | | ✔ | | ✔ | | ✔ |
| Telecommunications engineer | | ✔ | | | ✔ | ✔ | | ✔ |
| Telephonist | | ✔ | ✔ | | | ✔ | | ✔ |
| Television engineer | ✔ | | | ✔ | | ✔ | | ✔ |
| Television production assistant | | ✔ | ✔ | | | ✔ | | |
| Thatcher | | ✔ | | ✔ | | ✔ | | ✔ |
| Theatre administrator | | ✔ | | ✔ | | | ✔ | |
| Tiler | | ✔ | | ✔ | | ✔ | | ✔ |
| Tool maker | ✔ | | | ✔ | | ✔ | | ✔ |
| Toy maker | | ✔ | | ✔ | | | | |

# Personality Test and Job Satisfaction

| | F | I | S | D | A | P | G | So |
|---|---|---|---|---|---|---|---|---|
| Tracer | | ✔ | | ✔ | | ✔ | | |
| Traffic warden | ✔ | | | ✔ | | ✔ | | ✔ |
| Train driver | ✔ | | | ✔ | | ✔ | | ✔ |
| Training officer | | ✔ | | ✔ | | ✔ | | |
| Translator | | ✔ | ✔ | | | ✔ | | ✔ |
| Transport manager | ✔ | | ✔ | | ✔ | | | |
| Travel agent | | ✔ | | ✔ | | | | |
| Truck driver | | | | ✔ | | ✔ | | ✔ |
| Turf accountant | ✔ | | ✔ | | ✔ | | | |
| | | | | | | | | |
| Umpire | | | | ✔ | ✔ | | | ✔ |
| Underwriter | ✔ | | | ✔ | | ✔ | | |
| Union negotiator | | | | ✔ | ✔ | | | |
| Upholsterer | | ✔ | ✔ | | | ✔ | | ✔ |
| Urban planner | | ✔ | | ✔ | | ✔ | | |
| | | | | | | | | |
| Veterinary nurse | ✔ | | | ✔ | | ✔ | | |
| Veterinary surgeon | ✔ | | | ✔ | | | | |
| Vision mixer | | ✔ | | ✔ | | ✔ | | |
| Vocational counsellor | | ✔ | | | | ✔ | | |
| | | | | | | | | |
| Waiter/waitress | | ✔ | ✔ | | | ✔ | | |
| Watch repairer | | ✔ | | ✔ | | ✔ | | ✔ |
| Welder | ✔ | | | ✔ | | | | |
| Window dresser | | ✔ | ✔ | | | ✔ | | |
| Word processor operator | | ✔ | | ✔ | | ✔ | | |
| Work study officer | ✔ | | | ✔ | ✔ | | | ✔ |
| Writer | | ✔ | ✔ | | | | | ✔ |
| | | | | | | | | |
| Youth worker | | | | | | ✔ | ✔ | |
| | | | | | | | | |
| Zoo keeper | | ✔ | | | | | | ✔ |
| Zoologist | ✔ | | ✔ | | | ✔ | | ✔ |

# Part 3

# Motivation

# Chapter 11

# Career search test 1 – work activities

## Instructions

You are given three activities in each line of the test. You have to choose the one that appeals to you first, second and last. It is necessary to make a choice between all three so that a complete picture can be built up. Where you do not know what a particular career entails, it is a good idea to check in a careers library in a directory of occupations.

When looking at each set of three, simply write 1, 2 and 3 in the place provided, as in the example you are given on the next page. Sometimes you will find a set where the items are equally attractive or unattractive. Nevertheless, you have to make a choice in each case.

**Important:** The test seeks to establish what sorts of activities appeal to you. However, some people are concerned about how to respond if there is a distinction between what might appeal to them and what they think they are realistically capable of doing. There are two ways in which you can respond to the items in the test. Firstly, you could respond by asking yourself: 'Would I like to do this activity, regardless of whether I think I have the ability or qualifications?' This is generally the preferred method.

Secondly, you could respond by asking yourself: 'Would I like to do this activity and am I capable?' If you prefer to respond to the questionnaire in this way, that is perfectly all right; you can always do the questionnaire the other way later, using the first approach, if you wish.

Remember, also, that there is a danger of thinking you cannot do something when in fact you do have the hidden potential.

Above the sets of activities or jobs you have to choose between you will see the letters W, A, P, E, O, B and S. Ignore these for the time being. They will help with scoring your answers later on.

## Example

Place these titles in order of your preference:

| | | W | A | P | E | O | B | S |
|---|---|---|---|---|---|---|---|---|
| a) | Groom horses | | | a **3** | | | | |
| b) | Investigate causes of disease | | | | b **1** | | | |
| c) | Manage a small shop | | | | | | c **2** | |

In the example, investigating the causes of diseases is preferred most, then managing a small shop, while grooming horses is least preferred.

The test is done in just the same way. Begin when you are ready.

| | W | A | P | E | O | B | S |
|---|---|---|---|---|---|---|---|
| 1 a) Teach English as a foreign language | a | | | | | | |
| b) Decide upon framing and composition for filming | | b | | | | | |
| c) Replace car exhausts or tyres | | | c | | | | |

| | W | A | P | E | O | B | S |
|---|---|---|---|---|---|---|---|
| 2 a) Play in an orchestra | | a | | | | | |
| b) Repair corroded or damaged car panels | | | b | | | | |
| c) Identify remnants from ancient burial sites | | | | c | | | |

| | W | A | P | E | O | B | S |
|---|---|---|---|---|---|---|---|
| 3 a) Work with equipment to drill for oil on a floating platform | | | a | | | | |
| b) Use computers to approximate human intelligence | | | | b | | | |
| c) Work out insurance premiums to be paid | | | | | c | | |

| | | | | | | | |
|---|---|---|---|---|---|---|---|
| Leave this row blank until test is completed | | | | | | | |

| | W | A | P | E | O | B | S |
|---|---|---|---|---|---|---|---|
| 4 a) Study diseases of plants | | | | a | | | |
| b) Give advice about financial policies | | | | | b | | |
| c) Sell pop records | | | | | | c | |

| | W | A | P | E | O | B | S |
|---|---|---|---|---|---|---|---|
| 5 a) Estimate the cost of damage by fire or flood | | | | | a | | |
| b) Run an advertising promotion | | | | | | b | |
| c) Take responsibility for the care of patients | | | | | | | c |

| | W | A | P | E | O | B | S |
|---|---|---|---|---|---|---|---|
| 6 a) Translate speeches from one language to another | a | | | | | | |
| b) Design houses | | b | | | | | |
| c) Research how food can be preserved and stored | | | | c | | | |

| | W | A | P | E | O | B | S |
|---|---|---|---|---|---|---|---|
| Leave this row blank until test is completed | | | | | | | |

| | W | A | P | E | O | B | S |
|---|---|---|---|---|---|---|---|
| 7 a) Write music for TV commercials | | a | | | | | |
| b) Work from drawings to make engineering parts | | | b | | | | |
| c) Install telephones in domestic premises | | | | c | | | |

| | W | A | P | E | O | B | S |
|---|---|---|---|---|---|---|---|
| 8 a) Visit domestic premises to carry out service or repair to kitchen appliances | | | | a | | | |
| b) Study scientific journals to keep up to date with research | | | | | b | | |
| c  Direct the way a business is run | | | | | | | c |

| | W | A | P | E | O | B | S |
|---|---|---|---|---|---|---|---|
| 9 a) Study materials | | | | a | | | |
| b) Record details of stock transactions | | | | | b | | |
| c  Care for people who are mentally handicapped | | | | | | | c |

| | W | A | P | E | O | B | S |
|---|---|---|---|---|---|---|---|
| Leave this row blank until test is completed | | | | | | | |

**Test Yourself!**

|  | W | A | P | E | O | B | S |
|---|---|---|---|---|---|---|---|
| 10 a) Select the best articles for inclusion in a magazine | a | | | | | | |
| b) Draw cartoons for newspapers | | b | | | | | |
| c) Organise and cost supplies and services | | | | | c | | |

|  | W | A | P | E | O | B | S |
|---|---|---|---|---|---|---|---|
| 11 a) Talk to people about art | | a | | | | | |
| b) Use sheets of metal to make industrial objects | | | b | | | | |
| c) Seek election in order to represent others on a works council | | | | | | c | |

|  | W | A | P | E | O | B | S |
|---|---|---|---|---|---|---|---|
| 12 a) Devise a production programme in a factory | | | a | | | | |
| b) Take atmospheric readings with instruments and record data | | | | b | | | |
| c) Help mentally handicapped people | | | | | | | c |

| | W | A | P | E | O | B | S |
|---|---|---|---|---|---|---|---|
| Leave this row blank until test is completed | | | | | | | |

|  | W | A | P | E | O | B | S |
|---|---|---|---|---|---|---|---|
| 13 a) Develop new instruments to be placed in satellites for weather forecasting |  |  |  | a |  |  |  |
| b) Look for skilled people for hire by other businesses |  |  |  |  |  | b |  |
| c) Reassure and persevere with patients who are in pain |  |  |  |  |  |  | c |

|  | W | A | P | E | O | B | S |
|---|---|---|---|---|---|---|---|
| 14 a) Write a book about an historical figure | a |  |  |  |  |  |  |
| b) Communicate visually using drawings, prints and photographs |  | b |  |  |  |  |  |
| c) Open a small shop |  |  |  |  |  | c |  |

|  | W | A | P | E | O | B | S |
|---|---|---|---|---|---|---|---|
| 15 a) Design pottery or ornaments |  | a |  |  |  |  |  |
| b) Add finishing touches to a manufactured product |  | b |  |  |  |  |  |
| c) Help people to relax to assist well-being |  |  |  |  |  |  | c |

| Leave this row blank until test is completed |  |  |  |  |  |  |  |

| | W | A | P | E | O | B | S |
|---|---|---|---|---|---|---|---|
| 16 a) Ensure that appropriate materials are selected for the production of products | | | a | | | | |
| b) Compile documents relating to hospital patients | | | | | b | | |
| c) Be the head of a committee | | | | | | | c |

| | W | A | P | E | O | B | S |
|---|---|---|---|---|---|---|---|
| 17 a) Write a fictional account of an historical event | a | | | | | | |
| b) Design and make original articles of clothing | | b | | | | | |
| c) Educate people about their health and hygiene | | | | | | | c |

| Leave this row blank until test is completed | | | | | | | |
|---|---|---|---|---|---|---|---|

| | W | A | P | E | O | B | S |
|---|---|---|---|---|---|---|---|
| 18 a) Photograph weddings, sporting events and other occasions | | a | | | | | |
| b) Use statistical techniques to monitor the effects of contamination | | | | b | | | |
| c) Estimate the cost of rebuilding and painting damaged property | | | | | c | | |
| 19 a) Use tools to cut, punch and glue leather for use in crafts | | | a | | | | |
| b) Give legal or pensions advice | | | | | b | | |
| c) Help children who have a stammer | | | | | | | c |
| 20 a) Teach drama at a college | a | | | | | | |
| b) Spin or weave in order to produce textiles | | | b | | | | |
| c) Develop new telecommunication systems | | | | c | | | |
| Leave this row blank until test is completed | | | | | | | |

| | W | A | P | E | O | B | S |
|---|---|---|---|---|---|---|---|
| 21 a) Be responsible for the interior decoration of a boat | | a | | | | | |
| b) Study ancient documents | | | | b | | | |
| c) Collect commission on objects you had sold for people | | | | | | c | |

| | W | A | P | E | O | B | S |
|---|---|---|---|---|---|---|---|
| 22 a) Examine the way tasks are performed to increase efficiency | | | a | | | | |
| b) Run a house letting agency | | | | | | b | |
| c) Find families who may be suitable foster parents | | | | | | | c |

| | W | A | P | E | O | B | S |
|---|---|---|---|---|---|---|---|
| 23 a) Write scripts for radio programmes | a | | | | | | |
| b) Make specialist bread such as 'pitta' or 'croissants' | | | b | | | | |
| c) Prepare agendas and record minutes of meetings | | | | c | | | |

| | W | A | P | E | O | B | S |
|---|---|---|---|---|---|---|---|
| Leave this row blank until test is completed | | | | | | | |

| | W | A | P | E | O | B | S |
|---|---|---|---|---|---|---|---|
| 24 a) Write a book on painting and drawing technique | | a | | | | | |
| b) Write scientific textbooks | | | | b | | | |
| c) Meet parents to advise on options for employment or further training of their child | | | | | | | c |

| | W | A | P | E | O | B | S |
|---|---|---|---|---|---|---|---|
| 25 a) Take a part in a play | a | | | | | | |
| b) Make useful articles from pottery or metal | | | b | | | | |
| c) Manage a computer bureau | | | | | | c | |

| | W | A | P | E | O | B | S |
|---|---|---|---|---|---|---|---|
| 26 a) Design prints and posters | | a | | | | | |
| b) Advise clients about their tax liabilities | | | | | b | | |
| c) Sell kitchen equipment | | | | | | c | |

| | W | A | P | E | O | B | S |
|---|---|---|---|---|---|---|---|
| Leave this row blank until test is completed | | | | | | | |

| | W | A | P | E | O | B | S |
|---|---|---|---|---|---|---|---|
| 27 a) Teach English as a foreign language | a | | | | | | |
| b) Maintain factory machinery | | | b | | | | |
| c) Report on the best arrangement for the care and custody of children | | | | | | | c |

| | W | A | P | E | O | B | S |
|---|---|---|---|---|---|---|---|
| 28 a) Teach a course in modern art appreciation | | a | | | | | |
| b) Maintain stock control using a computer program | | | | | b | | |
| c) Look after the welfare of the elderly | | | | | | | c |

| | W | A | P | E | O | B | S |
|---|---|---|---|---|---|---|---|
| 29 a) Write a brochure for advertising a product or events | a | | | | | | |
| b) Listen to people with difficulties and advise upon behaviour | | | | b | | | |
| c) Submit a cost analysis for materials required for a project | | | | | c | | |

| | W | A | P | E | O | B | S |
|---|---|---|---|---|---|---|---|
| Leave this row blank until test is completed | | | | | | | |

|  | W | A | P | E | O | B | S |
|---|---|---|---|---|---|---|---|
| 30 a) Design fashion articles for the clothing industry |  | a |  |  |  |  |  |
| b) Be a manager in an insurance underwriting business |  |  |  |  |  | b |  |
| c) Run holiday activities for children |  |  |  |  |  |  | c |

| | W | A | P | E | O | B | S |
|---|---|---|---|---|---|---|---|
| 31 a) Read scripts for grammatical and spelling errors | a |  |  |  |  |  |  |
| b) Calculate wages for company employees |  |  |  | b |  |  |  |
| c) Buy articles for profitable resale |  |  |  |  |  | c |  |

| | W | A | P | E | O | B | S |
|---|---|---|---|---|---|---|---|
| 32 a) Write short articles for magazines | a |  |  |  |  |  |  |
| b) Research genetic material in a laboratory |  |  |  | b |  |  |  |
| c) Guide and advise holiday makers |  |  |  |  |  |  | c |

| | W | A | P | E | O | B | S |
|---|---|---|---|---|---|---|---|
| Leave this row blank until test is completed |  |  |  |  |  |  |  |

|  | W | A | P | E | O | B | S |
|---|---|---|---|---|---|---|---|
| 33 a) Write about local affairs for a newspaper | a |  |  |  |  |  |  |
| b) Prepare a report on the financial performance of a company |  |  |  |  | b |  |  |
| c) Buy property for commercial development |  |  |  |  |  | c |  |
| 34 a) Edit scripts prior to publication | a |  |  |  |  |  |  |
| b) Prepare tax returns for small businesses |  |  |  |  | b |  |  |
| c) Counsel people who have had emotional trauma |  |  |  |  |  |  | c |
| 35 a) Write a brochure explaining what a business is offering | a |  |  |  |  |  |  |
| b) Invest your money in a franchise business |  |  |  |  |  | b |  |
| c) Visit disadvantaged people to ensure they were being cared for |  |  |  |  |  |  | c |
| Leave this row blank until test is completed |  |  |  |  |  |  |  |

## Scoring

Step 1: Add column totals on each page of the test and place in the last box on each page. Place all page totals below:

|  | W | A | P | E | O | B | S |
|---|---|---|---|---|---|---|---|
| COLUMN TOTALS/all pages |  |  |  |  |  |  |  |

Step 2: Convert your score to a percentage (%) score, from the table given below:

| % |  | 100 | 95 | 90 | 85 | 80 | 75 | 70 | 65 | 60 | 55 |
|---|---|---|---|---|---|---|---|---|---|---|---|
| score |  | 15 | 16-17 | 18 | 19-20 | 21 | 22-23 | 24 | 25-26 | 27 | 28-29 |
|  |  |  |  |  |  |  |  |  |  |  |  |
| % |  | 50 | 45 | 40 | 35 | 30 | 25 | 20 | 15 | 10 | 5 |
| score |  | 30 | 31-32 | 33 | 34-35 | 36 | 37-38 | 39 | 40-41 | 42 | 43-45 |

For example, a score of 39 on W, or on any of the letters, would give a percentage score of 20. A score of 21 would give a percentage of 80.

Step 3: Place percentage scores in the columns:

|  | W | A | P | E | O | B | S |
|---|---|---|---|---|---|---|---|
| Percentage score (%) |  |  |  |  |  |  |  |

Step 4: Make a mark with a pen or pencil at the point on each of the radiating lines in the chart to show where your percentage score lies on each line.

Connect up each of the points on the graph. So, for the following percentage scores:

| | W | A | P | E | O | B | S |
|---|---|---|---|---|---|---|---|
| Percentage score (%) | 5 | 10 | 30 | 15 | 60 | 20 | 70 |

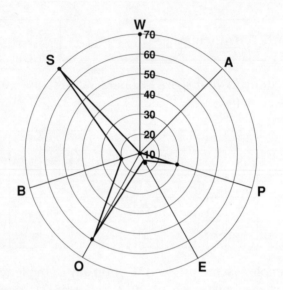

Note that the chart range ends at 70 per cent. This is because any score above this level will indicate a high level of interest. If you have a score that is higher than 70 per cent, you can extend the chart yourself, marking in your score as appropriate.

# Motivation and work activities chart

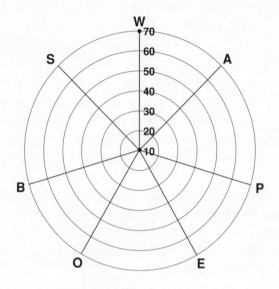

Here is what the letters mean:

| W | A | P | E | O | B | S |
|---|---|---|---|---|---|---|
| Words | Art | Physical | Experimental | Organizational | Business | Social |

# Interpreting the chart

The chart shows your areas of preferred and least preferred types of work activity.

The seven areas of work motivation form a scheme derived from three more fundamental areas: the Arts, the Sciences and the Humanities. The following is the scheme:

|        | ARTS  |     |          | SCIENCES     | HUMANITIES     |          |        |
|--------|-------|-----|----------|--------------|----------------|----------|--------|
| Social | Words | Art | Physical | Experimental | Organizational | Business | Social |
|        |       |     |          |              |                |          |        |

Your pattern of motivation forms a circle, so that each area flows into the next. Thus, Social can also appear in Arts. Words are used as an Art. Then, Art may also be visual or musical before it becomes a craft and more Physical. Then, the material, Physical area becomes more analytical or Experimenting in science. In turn, the scientific area becomes numerical and flows into finance and other areas of Organization. This leads into Business, then into the Social areas and, eventually, returns once again through communication to Words.

If you have a single high score, this will show very clearly where your motivation will be.

If there is another almost equally high score, or another strong score, you will probably want to have some chance of using this area of motivation in your work as well. Also, look at your lowest scores, because these are the least important to you, so you are unlikely to enjoy a career so much if it places undue emphasis upon these. It is usually possible to find a career that combines more than one area of motivation.

If your chart does not have any outstanding areas of interest, this will mean either that you are motivated by everything, or that none of the areas appeals to you at all!

A flat pattern of motivation does not have to be demotivating; perhaps you want a very broad job that involves you in some way with everything that is going on. In this case, it is probably a good idea to take the test again and this time be very strict with yourself about what is realistically possible for you. (In other words, take the test again using the second approach mentioned at the beginning of the chapter.) In such a situation, it may be wise to consult a careers counsellor. It is worth mentioning that, if you have not yet started work, it is a good idea to consult a careers counsellor in any case.

## Comparison of chart of motivation with careers titles

There are two charts for motivation in this book – one in this chapter, on work activities, the other being related to career titles. How much significance should be placed upon score differences between the two parts? A small percentage either way is perfectly understandable, but wide discrepancies would indicate that the activities appeal to you more than the careers themselves, or vice versa. For example, it would be as though you are rejecting the idea of certain jobs, but liking the sound of the nature of the work itself. This may be due to a lack of understanding of what the jobs actually involve.

It would therefore seem that, the greater your score differences, the weaker your perception of what is involved in that area of work. It might be worth doing some investigation as to what is involved in certain occupations you may be unclear about, especially if it is an area where you awarded 1 to some of the items in that area of motivation.

If you feel that one chart rather than the other gives a truer picture of your motivation, then use that one. You might prefer to do this if, for example, you consider that you understood all the activities perfectly well, but might have been confused by the job titles.

# Areas of motivation and courses of study

There follows a short description of the main areas of motivation. You can relate your motivation to different careers by looking up the corresponding section in the chapter on motivation and career titles. Many of the courses listed may have been placed under several of the headings. For example, Business Administration could appear under either Organization or Executive. Therefore, the category in which you find the courses is designed to give only general guidance.

You can relate your specific areas of motivation to specific jobs by referring to the careers guide at the end of the following chapter.

## W – Words

You will use words in your career whatever you do. In fact, you will already be an expert in the use of words simply from your experience of everyday living. However, if this is your high preference, it means that you want to make the business of words the means of making your living, not as an adjunct to some other activity.

You may have enjoyed English or other 'wordy' subjects, such as history, at school. Your aim may be to use words creatively or you may be drawn towards careers that in some way involve you with information and communication.

Few people have the talent to make a living on the basis of their creative writing. More structured and predictable careers arise in journalism or public relations. There are other careers that are often suited to this area of preference, such as legal work and librarianship.

## A – Art

A preference in this area almost invariably indicates that you want to use your imagination and express yourself through art, music or dance. At a deeper level, it can often suggest, even though a person may not be artistically gifted, that they want a career that allows them freedom and the opportunity to use their intuition.

Whatever form of art you pursue is likely to contain plenty of hard work and dedication. The discipline required by artists is frequently unappreciated by those outside artistic professions. Also, many careers in art are relatively lowly paid, which is surprising in view of the length of time needed to study for qualifications.

There are some people who are fortunate to become popular with comparatively little effort. So much in this area depends upon 'what the public wants' and whether you happen to be 'at the right place at the right time'.

Most creative careers do not carry any guarantees of security and income. Work may depend upon the piece of work you produce or may be linked to a short contract. More security of tenure exists if you work on a permanent basis as a member of a design team in a shop, with a manufacturer or in some other organization. These opportunities also give you a more continuing contact with others. This is an important point, since many artists are prepared to follow a style of life that requires a great deal of self-reliance.

## P – Physical

This area covers work where you might be physically active, perhaps engaged in sport or working outdoors. At one end of the spectrum, physical work might be delicate, even artistic, while at the other it might be heavy, involving large equipment or machinery. It might require skills that are visual as well as mechanical.

If you score highly in this area it is likely that you want to achieve something which is concrete. You might want to work by yourself on a task involving materials. Alternatively, you may want to use your experience and common sense in under-standing and interacting with the environment. In this case, you may want to work alone and be prepared to do so often under harsh, sometimes dangerous conditions.

## E – Experimental

What probably appeals to you about this area is the opportunity to acquire knowledge and to analyse results. These interests suit you to science since you enjoy observing, recording and making deductions.

Careers in this area require habits of study and precise work. An ability with mathematics is the common link with most, although, if your interest is biology, you may be less mathematically grounded than if your interest is physics. Work in all the sciences is changing as rapidly as technology changes, so that new opportunities for experimentation arise through increasingly powerful computers. Although science appears to be dependent upon instrumentation, it still requires the same enthusiastic curiosity.

Many areas of science are desperately short of qualified people, while in others it is difficult to get a job even with a higher degree.

## O – Organization

This area is about administration. It could include financial matters, as well as legal ones. It is relevant to all institutions whether in the public or private sector since it involves the effective use of resources whether of people or materials.

Since this area is concerned with making sure that decisions are carried out properly, you will need to be able to co-ordinate the efforts of others. Your own approach will need to be structured and orderly. People who organize, whether it is in a small office or a large enterprise, often have enormous influence, simply because they are the ones who know most about what is going on. As a consequence, such positions also carry a good deal of responsibility as well. This is why qualifications are increasingly sought in aspirants for senior positions. However, it is still possible to learn through experience and there is no doubt that if you have the right potential you will get on. In the larger organizations, senior positions are most likely to be occupied by people who have professional qualifications in banking, insurance, accountancy or similar.

## B – Business

If this is your highest preference you will be motivated by the chance to earn your living your own way. It is not about working by yourself, but working for yourself. This is true, even if your business is running somebody else's business on their behalf. Without a doubt, people who are most successful in this area run the business as if it were their own, whether it is or not. The responsibility and rewards for this type of career include all the attendant risks associated with failing to live up to the expectations people have of you and the specified or assumed promises you have made to them. For sure, in this career you are expected to have personal qualities of drive and determination.

The especially attractive feature of this area is that it is open to anybody, regardless of qualifications, though leaders of large businesses almost always seek to acquire qualifications in order to improve their performance further. Whatever the size of business you work in, being able to spot an opportunity, together with the will to succeed, are still the essential attributes.

## S – Social

Though every career involves contact with others at some point, your objective is to make people your focus. A high score in this area reveals how much you are prepared to assist others in their development. Your career may range from giving advice to devotedly caring for people who are unable to help themselves.

Such careers are seldom easy and sometimes require an extreme measure of personal resourcefulness. For example, social workers who have the best of intentions, sometimes have to make decisions on behalf of others which cause stress to everybody concerned, whether professional or client. Before entering a career in this area it is as well to gain experience to make sure it is right for you.

Success in this area depends upon personal judgement. Tact, patience and understanding are commodities you must have in abundance. A 'tough skin' is often required in situations where you may receive few thanks for your efforts. Of course, the rewards of seeing people improve make these careers worthwhile.

## Social and words

You will be interested in careers that combine ideas, people and communications. Obvious possibilities are in teaching, though other areas might involve you in some form of business, for example, public relations.

If you are more concerned with the literary side, then language skills may be more important to you than the caring, social side. On the other hand, a speech therapist may have skills in linguistics, though the primary aim is to help others overcome difficulties rather than acquire knowledge.

## Words and art

You appear to seek knowledge and the chance to express ideas, often in novel ways. It is unlikely that you will be satisfied by a more conventional career. Therefore, the way you work and what you do will often be admired by others who will admire the variety and lifestyle you appear to have. Such careers are not without risk, so perhaps the most important asset to have is a belief in yourself and what you are doing.

### Art and physical
This area gives you the chance to apply art in a practical way. An example would be the potter, whose sense of proportion and design is wedded to a useful object. There are many crafts that combine beauty with practicality.

There are also attendant opportunities if you look beyond the task itself. For example, your talent might lead to a business, or it could take you into the social area, through teaching or therapy.

### Physical and experimental
This area will involve you with the application of science. You are the person who takes the theory and makes it work in practice. Such careers demand knowledge and experience. Often, people rely upon you more than they know, and what you do is essential to a secure and comfortable existence.

### Experimenting and organizational
You may be interested in mathematics, statistics, finance or marketing, and other areas that combine your interest in figures with an analytical approach. If your interest is statistics, you are more likely to be on the scientific side. If your interest veers more towards the actuarial, then you will probably prefer to work in a business organization.

Careers which combine the two areas very well indeed, and where there are expanding opportunities, are in systems areas. It is possible to be involved with systems integration as well as systems development within an organization. In these cases,

you would be expected to have skills on the social side as
well.

## Organizational and business

You are likely to be astute and commercially minded. You will
enjoy the thought of working within organizations such as
banking, insurance, finance and administration. You will need to
be a good manager, first of all in managing the efforts of others
and also in managing systems and resources. Whereas many
business-minded people are quite intuitive, you are more
controlled and factual. Your knowledge about how business
works together with your drive for efficiency is likely to mean
you are a force to be reckoned with.

## Business and social

You will want to work with and for people, but not in a
personal, caring way. Instead, your efforts are likely to be more
detached, though, sometimes, on a grander scale. Thus, you
might achieve a great deal for others through your business
sense. You may show your concern by creating the circumstances or the resources through which others are enabled to
care in a more direct way. You are more likely to head the
committee that obtains the resources that patients need than be
a skilled helper yourself. Your obvious talents are more likely to
be political than sensitive, though there is no doubt that the
latter is present as well.

## Social and art

Careers that combine these areas require skills in relation to the
subject and skills in relation to people. A great deal of sympathy,
warmth and patience is required in order to communicate with
others and help them. Many careers in this area are undertaken
by volunteers, who often have extensive experience and insight

to bring to their work. This is unlikely to be the correct area for you if your aim is to do great things with your art. Instead, you would want to use your subject in the service of others, a very selfless activity.

## Social and physical

You would want to be active, working with others in order to achieve a definite task. Your tendency is to 'go for it'. The way you approach your work will depend upon whether you are something of an organiizer or whether you are more artistic. In the former case, you may be drawn to areas of industrial production. In the latter case, you may enjoy sports coaching or aerobics teaching. If your other, supporting interests are more towards business, then you may like to be in charge of some team work or operation management. Your enthusiasm and ability to work with others usually mean that you will be an effective leader.

## Social and experimenting

If these are your interests, you will probably want to apply expert knowledge in the service of others. You may well be consulted for advice, but your relationship with others is more likely to be professional and detached than emotionally involved. Your background will be in science, but your intention will be to direct that science to others' welfare or education.

## Words and physical

These two areas are generally mutually exclusive; although most of us are active and communicating with each other most of the time, there are few careers that combine them specifically. The writer of technical books or the sports writer are examples which show how the two can come together, but these are very highly specialized careers indeed. How can you get started? It will be worth looking at the words and physical areas separately, at the same time thinking whether any careers in these areas will give you enough scope for your other interest. Also, consult the career index where some other alternatives may be found.

### Art and experimental

You will want scope in your career to combine your interests in an expressive medium as well as to analyse. Clearly, you have a desire to use science and technology to create something of perfection. You may well come up with some innovative ideas yourself. It seems that whatever work you do, some creative or technical challenge is important.

### Physical and organizational

If these are your interests, then you will want a career that requires you to implement and get things done. You probably like to work in a moving environment. You may like to be 'out and about' yourself. Ensuring that resources, goods or equipment are getting to the right place at the right time is something that you will be interested in. Increasingly, careers in this area will involve you in costing and budgeting in order that deadlines can be completed on schedule.

### Physical and business

You want to combine an interest in business with the chance to be out and about, or become actively involved with what is happening. You may like to be on a site or involved with property. You might enjoy buying and selling equipment or stock. Typically, you will be practically minded, making things happen or turning your hand to most things.

### Experimental and business

These preferences seek to combine the intellectual with the

material. It is sometimes possible, as is shown by the number of chemists (pharmacists) who venture into retail. Of course, science is big business, so many of the largest companies, such as drug companies, have huge teams of scientific researchers. Those who make it to the top of these organizations start out in science, but have developed a strong streak of business enterprise along the way.

Your interests lie in the realm of ideas, communication and intellectual challenge. You will like to acquire knowledge for which you may perceive novel applications. You may lack the practicality to turn ideas into reality, but you may inspire others to do so.

## Organizational and social

You want to work with others as part of an efficient team. People may well look to you for leadership, since you appear willing to do the necessary paperwork and scheduling. Although your administrative and personal skills may be useful in most organizations, particularly in business, you seem likely to derive most satisfaction when your work has an altruistic element. You work well in a community or in public institutions where you experience a sense of purpose from assisting others.

It may be that you enjoyed literary subjects at school, but decided that you were more commercially minded than academic. Broadly, your preferences will direct you towards careers that are administrative. You will no doubt be involved with communications and probably the management of others as well. These careers may not have much in the way of a literary or creative content, but may have great variety and scope for expression in a practical way.

## Organizational and art

You are seeking a creative environment as well as responsibility for getting things done. You might enjoy working in a fast-paced, hectic job where the end result nevertheless has to be a superb performance

## Business and words
Your own background might be literary and you might enjoy writing yourself. However, your greater interest is to combine your interest in books and ideas in business. Also, you might be drawn to a career where you are 'in the spotlight'. In this case, your career might be connected with communications.

## Business and art
These preferences almost always signify a desire to have a varied, enterprising career. You will enjoy a career that involves you with design or with the media. You like ideas and will seek opportunities for some original expression. You will probably be quick to spot something, which is material or an idea, that will appeal to others. Often, you can arrange these things in a way that demonstrates the appeal of what you have discovered.

# Chapter 12

# Career search test 2 – career titles

## Instructions

This test follows exactly the same format as the previous test on work activities. The difference is that this one presents you with distinct occupations.

You are given three careers in each line of the test. You have to choose the one that appeals to you first, second and last. It is necessary to make a choice between all three so that a complete picture can be built up.

When looking at each set of three, simply write 1, 2 and 3 in the place provided, as in the example you are given on the next page. Sometimes you will find a set where the items are equally attractive or unattractive. Nevertheless, you have to make a choice in each case.

**Important:** The test seeks to establish what career areas appeal to you. However, some people are concerned about how to respond if there is a distinction between what might appeal to them and what they think they are realistically capable of doing. There are two ways in which you can respond to the items in the test. Firstly, you could respond by asking yourself:

'Would I like to do this career, regardless of whether I think I have the ability or qualifications?' This is generally the preferred method.

Secondly, you could respond by asking yourself: 'Would I like to do this job and am I capable?' If you prefer to respond to the test in this way, that is perfectly all right; you can always do the test the other way later, using the first approach, if you wish.

Remember also that there is a danger of thinking you cannot do something when in fact you do have the hidden potential.

Above the sets of activities or jobs you have to choose between you will see the letters W, A, P, E, O, B and S. Ignore these for the time being. They will help with scoring your answers later on.

## Example

Place these jobs in order of your preference:

|  |  | W | A | P | E | O | B | S |
|---|---|---|---|---|---|---|---|---|
| a) | Animal worker | | | a **3** | | | | |
| b) | Laboratory Assistant | | | | b **1** | | | |
| c) | Chemist's shop owner | | | | | | c **2** | |

In the example, being a laboratory assistant is preferred most, then owning a chemist's shop, while being an animal worker is least preferred.

The test is done in just the same way. Begin when you are ready.

|  | W | A | P | E | O | B | S |
|---|---|---|---|---|---|---|---|
| 1 a) Journalist | a |  |  |  |  |  |  |
| b) Architect |  | b |  |  |  |  |  |
| c) Security guard |  |  | c |  |  |  |  |
| 2 a) Dress maker |  | a |  |  |  |  |  |
| b) Gym instructor |  |  | b |  |  |  |  |
| c) Geophysicist |  |  |  | c |  |  |  |
| 3 a) Bus driver |  |  | a |  |  |  |  |
| b) Dietician |  |  |  | b |  |  |  |
| c) Administrative assistant |  |  |  |  | c |  |  |
| 4 a) Medical technical officer |  |  |  | a |  |  |  |
| b) Call centre adviser |  |  |  |  | b |  |  |
| c) Business person |  |  |  |  |  | c |  |
| 5 a) Arrange loans for banking customers |  |  |  |  | a |  |  |
| b) Market research executive |  |  |  |  |  | b |  |
| c) Hospital nurse |  |  |  |  |  |  | c |
| 6 a) Copy writer | a |  |  |  |  |  |  |
| b) Sculptor |  | b |  |  |  |  |  |
| c) Medical laboratory scientist |  |  |  | c |  |  |  |
| Leave this row blank until test is completed |  |  |  |  |  |  |  |

|  | W | A | P | E | O | B | S |
|---|---|---|---|---|---|---|---|
| 7 a) Sign writer |  | a |  |  |  |  |  |
| b) Tree pruner (Arborist) |  |  | b |  |  |  |  |
| c) Purchasing officer |  |  |  |  | c |  |  |
| 8 a) Barperson |  |  | a |  |  |  |  |
| b) Computer systems programmer |  |  |  | b |  |  |  |
| c) Commodity broker |  |  |  |  |  | c |  |
| 9 a) Ecologist |  |  |  | a |  |  |  |
| Business statistician |  |  |  |  | b |  |  |
| Teacher of the blind |  |  |  |  |  |  | c |
| 10 a) Actor/actress | a |  |  |  |  |  |  |
| b) Furniture designer |  | b |  |  |  |  |  |
| c) Post office clerical worker |  |  |  |  | c |  |  |
| 11 a) Graphic designer |  | a |  |  |  |  |  |
| b) Window cleaner |  |  | b |  |  |  |  |
| c) Head of a charity |  |  |  |  |  | c |  |
| 12 a) Building worker |  |  | a |  |  |  |  |
| b) Orthodontist |  |  |  | b |  |  |  |
| c) Osteopath |  |  |  |  |  |  | c |
| Leave this row blank until test is completed |  |  |  |  |  |  |  |

|  | W | A | P | E | O | B | S |
|---|---|---|---|---|---|---|---|
| 13 a) Biochemist |  |  |  | a |  |  |  |
| b) Antique dealer |  |  |  |  |  | b |  |
| c) Drugs counsellor |  |  |  |  |  |  | c |
| 14 a) Film critic | a |  |  |  |  |  |  |
| b) Jewellery designer |  | b |  |  |  |  |  |
| c) Art dealer |  |  |  |  |  | c |  |
| 15 a) Choral singer |  | a |  |  |  |  |  |
| b) Jockey |  |  | b |  |  |  |  |
| c) Educational psychologist |  |  |  |  |  |  | c |
| 16 a) Production manager |  |  | a |  |  |  |  |
| b) Company secretary |  |  |  |  | b |  |  |
| c) Merchant banker |  |  |  |  |  | c |  |
| 17 a) Linguist | a |  |  |  |  |  |  |
| b) Organist |  | b |  |  |  |  |  |
| c) Prison officer |  |  |  |  |  |  | c |
| 18 a) Member of a music band |  | a |  |  |  |  |  |
| b) Scientific instrument technician |  |  |  | b |  |  |  |
| c) Legal assistant |  |  |  |  | c |  |  |
| Leave this row blank until test is completed |  |  |  |  |  |  |  |

**Test Yourself!**

| | W | A | P | E | O | B | S |
|---|---|---|---|---|---|---|---|
| 19 a) Member of a lifeboat crew | | | a | | | | |
| b) Purchasing officer | | | | | b | | |
| c) Residential social worker | | | | | | | c |
| 20 a) Children's author | a | | | | | | |
| b) Traffic warden | | | b | | | | |
| c) Doctor of medicine | | | | c | | | |
| 21 a) Book cover/poster artist | | a | | | | | |
| b) Veterinary surgeon | | | | b | | | |
| c) Property dealer | | | | | | c | |
| 22 a) Gun maker | | | a | | | | |
| b) Hotel owner | | | | | | b | |
| c) Careers adviser | | | | | | | c |
| 23 a) Librarian | a | | | | | | |
| b) Truck driver | | | b | | | | |
| c) Court reporter | | | | | c | | |
| 24 a) Photographer | | a | | | | | |
| b) Astronomer | | | | b | | | |
| c) Naturopath | | | | | | | c |
| Leave this row blank until test is completed | | | | | | | |

|  | W | A | P | E | O | B | S |
|---|---|---|---|---|---|---|---|
| 25 a) Advertising copy writer | a | | | | | | |
| b) Cook | | | b | | | | |
| c) Publicity agent | | | | | | c | |
| 26 a) Window dresser | | a | | | | | |
| b) Invoice payments manager | | | | | b | | |
| c) Account manager | | | | | | c | |
| 27 a) Bookseller | a | | | | | | |
| b) Electrical engineer | | | b | | | | |
| c) Children's nurse | | | | | | | c |
| 28 a) Interior decorator | | a | | | | | |
| b) Trading standards officer | | | | | b | | |
| c) Remedial teacher | | | | | | | c |
| 29 a) Local newspaper reporter | a | | | | | | |
| b) Pharmacist | | | b | | | | |
| c) Statistician | | | | | c | | |
| 30 a) Art restorer | | a | | | | | |
| b) Management consultant | | | | | | b | |
| c) Physiotherapist | | | | | | | c |
| Leave this row blank until test is completed | | | | | | | |

|  | W | A | P | E | O | B | S |
|---|---|---|---|---|---|---|---|
| 31 a) Technical author | a | | | | | | |
| b) Anthropologist | | | | b | | | |
| c) Shop owner | | | | | | c | |

|  | W | A | P | E | O | B | S |
|---|---|---|---|---|---|---|---|
| 32 a) Newsreader | a | | | | | | |
| b) Bacteriologist | | | | b | | | |
| c) Youth club leader | | | | | | | c |

|  | W | A | P | E | O | B | S |
|---|---|---|---|---|---|---|---|
| 33 a) Proof reader | a | | | | | | |
| b) Tax adviser | | | | | b | | |
| c) Insurance salesperson | | | | | | c | |

|  | W | A | P | E | O | B | S |
|---|---|---|---|---|---|---|---|
| 34 a) Language teacher | a | | | | | | |
| b) Banking adviser | | | | | b | | |
| c) Teacher of the deaf | | | | | | | c |

|  | W | A | P | E | O | B | S |
|---|---|---|---|---|---|---|---|
| 35 a) Television programme researcher | a | | | | | | |
| b) Share trader | | | | | | b | |
| c) Social worker | | | | | | | c |

| | W | A | P | E | O | B | S |
|---|---|---|---|---|---|---|---|
| Leave this row blank until test is completed | | | | | | | |

## Scoring

Step 1: Add column totals on each page of the test and place in the last box on each page. Place all page totals below:

|  | W | A | P | E | O | B | S |
|---|---|---|---|---|---|---|---|
| COLUMN TOTALS/all pages |  |  |  |  |  |  |  |

Step 2: Convert your score to a percentage (%) score, from the table given below:

| % |  | 100 | 95 | 90 | 85 | 80 | 75 | 70 | 65 | 60 | 55 |
|---|---|---|---|---|---|---|---|---|---|---|---|
| score |  | 15 | 16-17 | 18 | 19-20 | 21 | 22-23 | 24 | 25-26 | 27 | 28-29 |
|  |  |  |  |  |  |  |  |  |  |  |  |
| % |  | 50 | 45 | 40 | 35 | 30 | 25 | 20 | 15 | 10 | 5 |
| score |  | 30 | 31-32 | 33 | 34-35 | 36 | 37-38 | 39 | 40-41 | 42 | 43-45 |

For example, a score of 15 on W, or on any of the letters, would give a percentage score of 100. A score of 21 would give a percentage of 80. A score of 44 would give a percentage of 5.

Step 3: Place percentage scores in the columns:

|  | W | A | P | E | O | B | S |
|---|---|---|---|---|---|---|---|
| Percentage score (%) |  |  |  |  |  |  |  |

Step 4: Make a mark with a pen or pencil at the point on the chart to show where your percentage score lies on each line. Connect up each of the points. For example, for the following percentage scores:

| | W | A | P | E | O | B | S |
|---|---|---|---|---|---|---|---|
| Percentage score (%) | 15 | 10 | 90 | 5 | 60 | 20 | 10 |

The chart would look like this:

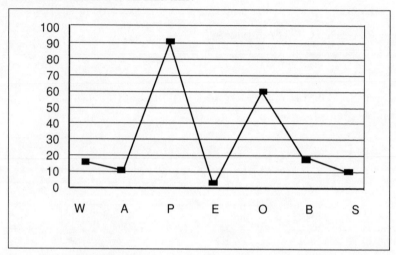

## Motivation and careers chart

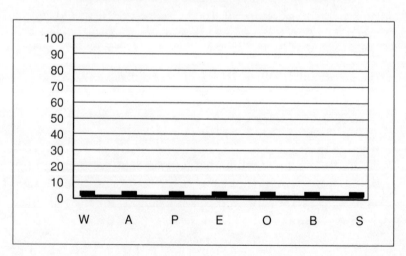

This is what the letters mean:

| W | A | P | E | O | B | S |
|---|---|---|---|---|---|---|
| Words | Art | Physical | Experimental | Organizational | Business | Social |

# Interpreting the chart

This is exactly the same as the previous chapter (pp 203) except that we are now dealing with careers as opposed to work activities. If you have not already read this section in the previous chapter, it would be advisable to do so now. Also read the following section (pp 204) before returning to the careers guide below.

# Careers guide

If you have more than a single strong area of interest, try to find a way to involve all of your interests in a career. Although it is often necessary to specialize, there are often opportunities to 'bolt on' other interests to your main career. For example, an architect may have a strong interest in the Art area, but some architects may also be interested in involving themselves in Business and Organization. Similarly, an accountant is likely to have a strong interest in the Organization area. If there is also an interest in the Social area, it may be possible to take responsibility for human resources matters within an accounting business. If there is an interest in the Physical area, it may be possible to work out of doors, perhaps in quantity surveying, or work in an organization that deals with products, equipment or machines.

**Test Yourself!**

The examples that are given below are those that often correspond with an area of interest.

*W – Words*
actor/actress
advertising copywriter
bilingual secretary
book critic
creative writer
editor
historian
interpreter
journalist
language teacher
librarian
literary critic
proof-reader

*A – Art*
architect
artist
dancer
dressmaker
engraver
florist
goldsmith
illustrator
interior designer
make-up artist
musician
sculptor
silversmith
vision mixer
window dresser

*P – Physical*
agricultural mechanic
animal handler
appliance repairer
automobile technician
baker
blacksmith/farrier
boat builder
builder
butcher
carpenter
coast guard
cook
diver
driver
farmer
fisherman
fitter
forester
gamekeeper
groom
groundsman
guard
gunsmith
instrument maker
jockey
joiner
lighthouse keeper
locksmith
mechanic
merchant seaman
miner
nature conservancy warden

oil rig worker
park ranger
plumber
shipping pilot
traffic warden
upholsterer
veterinary nurse

*E – Experimenting*
astronomer
audiology technician
bacteriologist
botanist
chemist
dietician
ergonomist
experimental psychologist
forensic scientist
laboratory technician
materials scientist
mathematician
meteorologist
microbiologist
ophthalmologist
physicist
radiographer
surgeon
zoologist

*O – Organization*
accountant
accounting technician
actuary

administrator
auditor
bank clerk
bursar
cashier
clerk
company secretary
fund manager/assistant
legal executive
purser
records clerk
securities analyst
tax inspector

## B – Business
broker
business consultant
business person
exporter/importer
management consultant
managing director
marketing manager
negotiator
personnel director
political agent
politician
retail manager
sales manager

## S – Social
ambulance crew
careers adviser
child-care officer

chiropodist
educational psychologist
health visitor
hostel warden
industrial nurse
medical practitioner
midwife
nurse
nursery nurse
osteopath
physiotherapist
probation officer
remedial teacher
social worker
teacher

*Social and words*
drama teacher
interviewer
language teacher
liberal studies teacher
psychoanalyst
speech therapist
training officer

*Words and art*
actor/actress
advertising copywriter
dramatist
film director
film reviewer
TV production assistant
voice-over

*Art and physical*
bookbinder
cabinet maker
cake maker
camera person
confectioner
curtain maker
dresser
embalmer
emboiderer
flyperson
gardener
pattern cutter
pattern maker
picture framer
potter

*Physical and experimenting*
agriculturist
biomedical engineer
computer engineer
engineer
- aeronautical
- civil
- mechanical
- production
environmental health officer
ergonomist
geologist
horologist
hydrologist
instrument maker
metallurgist

navigating officer
surveyor
technologist
work study officer

## Experimenting and organizing
business systems analyst
chief actuary
computer programmer
economist
market researcher
operations researcher
statistician
systems analyst

## Organizing and business
bank manager
club manaer
estate manager
insurance manager
office manager
tax consultant
turf accountant
underwriter

## Business and social
charity manager
funeral director
head teacher
hospital manager
hotel manager
job interviewer
retail manager

sales person
social services director

*Social and art*
aromatherapist
art teacher
art therapist
beautician
dance instructor
masseur/masseuse
music therapist
nursery teacher
occupational therapist
piano teacher
waiter/waitress

*Social and physical*
hairdresser
masseur/masseuse
occupational therapist
police officer
prison officer
production supervisor
sports coach/assistant
team coach
youth leader

*Social and experimenting*
clinical psychologist
dental assistant
dentist
nurse
orthoptist

radiographer
science teacher
social science researcher

*Words and physical*
printer
secretary in agriculture
sports writer
technical writer

*Art and experimenting*
archaeologist
beautician
car stylist
cartographer
designer
fine art restorer
lighting technician
medical illustrator
museum assistant
photographer

*Physical and organizing*
baths manager
builder's merchant
customs officer
manufacturing team leader
logistics manager/transport manager
office machinery mechanic
organization and methods officer
rating valuation officer
works manager

*Physical and business*
accident assessor
auctioneer
demonstrator
domestic engineering manager
estate agent
farm manager
production manager
publican
undertaker

*Experimenting and business*
computer consultant
director of scientific research company
dispensing optician
medical representative
retail pharmacist
technical representative
veterinary surgeon

*Experimenting and words*
anthropologist
archaeologist
information scientist
market researcher
science writer
technical writer

*Organizing and social*
courier/local representative
employment officer
medical secretary
principal nursing officer

**Test Yourself!**

## Organizing and words
administrator (clerical/executive)
barrister
company secretary
entertainment officer
legal executive
library assistant
receptionist
secretary
solicitor

## Organizing and art
box office clerk
chef
choreographer
cinema manager
front of house manager
merchandiser
props manager
receptionist
studio assistant
theatre administrator
wardrobe manager

## Business and words
conference executive
literary agent
newspaper editor/manager
pubic relations executive
publisher
radio, TV or film producer

*Business and art*
advertising account executive
art dealer
brand manager
fashion buyer
media director
sales person

## Career search questionnaires and career profile

The career profile allows you a means of checking how your interests may relate to certain careers. The profile is not meant to be exact, only to serve as a basis for you to think through whether what you choose to do seems to fit well with your underlying motivation as revealed by either of the two career search tests.

The results on either of the career search questionnaires may be used.

# Career search profiles and careers

Code

| | |
|---|---|
| W | Words |
| A | Art |
| P | Practical |
| E | Experimenting |
| O | Organizing |
| B | Business |
| S | Social |

| | W | A | P | E | O | B | S |
|---|---|---|---|---|---|---|---|
| Accident assessor | | | ✔ | | ✔ | | |
| Accountant | | | | | ✔ | ✔ | |
| Accounting technician | | | | | ✔ | | |
| Actor | ✔ | ✔ | | | | | |
| Actuary | | | | ✔ | ✔ | | |
| Acupuncturist | | ✔ | | ✔ | | | ✔ |
| Administrator | ✔ | | | | ✔ | | |
| Advertising copywriter | ✔ | | | | | | |
| Advertising executive | ✔ | | | | | ✔ | |
| Aerobics instructor | | ✔ | ✔ | | | | ✔ |
| Aeronautical engineer | | | ✔ | ✔ | | | |
| Aeronautical technician | | | ✔ | ✔ | | | |
| Agriculturalist | | | ✔ | ✔ | | | |
| Agricultural mechanic | | | ✔ | | | | |
| Agricultural secretary | ✔ | | ✔ | | | | |
| Air hostess | | ✔ | ✔ | | | | ✔ |
| Air traffic controller | | | ✔ | ✔ | | | |
| Ambulance crew | | | ✔ | | | | ✔ |
| Anaesthetist | | | | ✔ | | | ✔ |
| Animal keeper | | | ✔ | | | | |
| Animal nurse | | | ✔ | | | | |
| Anthropologist | ✔ | ✔ | | ✔ | | | |
| Antique dealer | | ✔ | | | | ✔ | |
| Appliance repairer | | | ✔ | | | | |

| | W | A | P | E | O | B | S |
|---|---|---|---|---|---|---|---|
| Arborist | | ✔ | ✔ | | | | |
| Architect | | ✔ | | | | | |
| Architectural technician | | ✔ | | | | | |
| Archivist | ✔ | | | | ✔ | | |
| Armed forces officer | | | ✔ | | | ✔ | ✔ |
| Armed forces personnel | | | ✔ | | | | ✔ |
| Aromatherapist | | ✔ | | | | | ✔ |
| Art dealer | | ✔ | | | | ✔ | |
| Artist | | ✔ | | | | | |
| Art restorer | | ✔ | | ✔ | | | |
| Arts adminstrator | ✔ | ✔ | | | ✔ | | |
| Art therapist | | ✔ | | | | | ✔ |
| Astronaut | | | ✔ | ✔ | | | |
| Astronomer | | | | ✔ | | | |
| Auctioneer | | | | | ✔ | | |
| Audiology technician | | | | ✔ | | | |
| Auditor | | | | | ✔ | | |
| Author | ✔ | | | | | | |
| Automobile technician | | | ✔ | | | | |
| | | | | | | | |
| Bacteriologist | | | | ✔ | | | |
| Baggage handler | | | ✔ | | | | |
| Baker | | ✔ | | | | | |
| Ballet dancer | | ✔ | | | | | |
| Bank clerk | | | | | ✔ | | |
| Bank manager | | | | | ✔ | ✔ | |
| Barperson | | | ✔ | | | | |
| Barrister | ✔ | | | | | ✔ | |
| Beautician | | ✔ | | | | | ✔ |
| Bicycle repairer | | | ✔ | | | | |
| Bilingual secretary | ✔ | | | | | | |
| Biologist | | | | ✔ | | | |
| Biomedical engineer | | | ✔ | ✔ | | | |
| Blacksmith/farrier | | | ✔ | | | | |
| Boatbuilder | | ✔ | ✔ | | | | |
| Bookbinder | | ✔ | | | | | |
| Book critic | ✔ | | | | | | |

**Test Yourself!**

| | W | A | P | E | O | B | S |
|---|---|---|---|---|---|---|---|
| Book illustrator | ✓ | | | | | | |
| Bookseller | | | | | ✓ | | |
| Botanist | | | ✓ | | | | |
| Brewer | | ✓ | ✓ | | | | |
| Bricklayer | | ✓ | | | | | |
| Broker | | | | | ✓ | | |
| Builder's merchant | | | | ✓ | | | |
| Building demolition expert | | ✓ | | | | | |
| Building inspector | | ✓ | | ✓ | | | |
| Building society assistant | | | ✓ | | | | |
| Building society manager | | | ✓ | ✓ | | | |
| Building surveyor | ✓ | ✓ | | | | | |
| Bursar | | | ✓ | | | | |
| Bus driver | | ✓ | | | | | |
| Business consultant | | | | | ✓ | | |
| Buyer | ✓ | | | | ✓ | | |
| | | | | | | | |
| Cabinet maker | ✓ | | | | | | |
| Camera repairer | | ✓ | | | | | |
| Car body designer | ✓ | | | | | | |
| Careers adviser | | | | | | | ✓ |
| Carpenter | ✓ | | | | | | |
| Cartographer | ✓ | | | | | | |
| Cartoon animator | ✓ | | | | | | |
| Cashier | | | | ✓ | | | |
| Caterer | ✓ | | | ✓ | | | |
| CD-ROM producer | ✓ | | | | ✓ | | |
| Chef | ✓ | | | | | | |
| Chemical technician | | | ✓ | | | | |
| Chemical technologist | | | ✓ | | | | |
| Chemist | | | ✓ | | | | |
| Chief executive | | | | ✓ | | | |
| Child care worker | | | | | | | ✓ |
| Chimney sweep | | ✓ | | | | | |
| Chiropodist | | | ✓ | | | | ✓ |
| Choreographer | ✓ | | | | | | |
| Cinema manager | ✓ | | | | ✓ | | |

|                              | W | A | P | E | O | B | S |
|------------------------------|---|---|---|---|---|---|---|
| Civil engineer               |   |   | ✔ | ✔ |   |   |   |
| Civil servant                |   |   |   | ✔ |   |   |   |
| Clerk                        |   |   | ✔ |   |   |   |   |
| Clinical psychologist        |   |   | ✔ |   |   |   | ✔ |
| Clown                        |   | ✔ |   |   |   |   |   |
| Club manager                 |   |   |   |   | ✔ |   |   |
| Coastguard                   |   | ✔ |   |   |   |   |   |
| College admissions counsellor |  |   |   |   | ✔ |   | ✔ |
| Comic illustrator            |   | ✔ |   |   |   |   |   |
| Commercial account manager   |   |   |   | ✔ | ✔ |   |   |
| Community social worker      |   |   |   |   |   |   | ✔ |
| Community warden             |   |   |   |   |   |   | ✔ |
| Company secretary            | ✔ |   |   |   | ✔ |   |   |
| Compositor                   |   | ✔ |   |   |   |   |   |
| Computer animator            |   | ✔ |   | ✔ |   |   |   |
| Computer game designer       |   | ✔ |   |   |   |   |   |
| Computer hardware designer   |   |   | ✔ | ✔ |   |   |   |
| Computer systems analyst     |   |   | ✔ | ✔ |   |   |   |
| Computer technician          |   |   | ✔ | ✔ |   |   |   |
| Confectioner                 |   | ✔ |   |   |   |   |   |
| Conference organizer         |   | ✔ |   |   | ✔ |   |   |
| Conservation officer         |   | ✔ |   | ✔ |   |   |   |
| Copywriter                   | ✔ |   |   |   |   |   |   |
| Coroner                      | ✔ |   |   | ✔ |   |   |   |
| Cost accountant              |   |   |   |   | ✔ |   |   |
| Counsellor                   |   |   |   |   |   |   | ✔ |
| Courier                      |   | ✔ |   |   |   |   |   |
| Court reporter               | ✔ |   |   |   |   |   |   |
| Crane operator               |   |   | ✔ |   |   |   |   |
| Criminologist                | ✔ |   |   |   |   |   |   |
| Cruise director              |   |   |   |   |   | ✔ |   |
| Cryptographer                | ✔ |   |   |   |   |   |   |
| Cultural anthropologist      | ✔ | ✔ |   | ✔ |   |   |   |
| Curator                      | ✔ | ✔ |   |   |   |   |   |
| Currency trader              |   |   |   |   |   | ✔ |   |

# Test Yourself!

| | W | A | P | E | O | B | S |
|---|---|---|---|---|---|---|---|
| Customer services manager | | | | | ✓ | | ✓ |
| Customs officer | | | ✓ | | ✓ | | |
| Dance instructor | | ✓ | | | | | ✓ |
| Dancer | | ✓ | | | | | |
| Deaf interpreter | | | | | | | ✓ |
| Decorator | | ✓ | | | | | |
| Demonstrator | | | | | | ✓ | |
| Dental assistant | | | | ✓ | | | ✓ |
| Dental hygienist | | | | ✓ | | | ✓ |
| Dental nurse | | | | ✓ | | | ✓ |
| Dental technician | | | ✓ | ✓ | | | |
| Dentist | | | | ✓ | | | ✓ |
| Dermatologist | | | | ✓ | | | |
| Design engineer | | ✓ | | | | | |
| Designer | | ✓ | | | | | |
| Dietician | | | | ✓ | | | |
| Director (media) | ✓ | ✓ | | | ✓ | | |
| Disc jockey | | ✓ | | | | | |
| Dispensing optician | | | | ✓ | ✓ | | |
| Display artist | | ✓ | | | | | |
| Diver | | | ✓ | | | | |
| Doctor of medicine | | | | ✓ | | | ✓ |
| Drama teacher | ✓ | | | | | | ✓ |
| Draughtsperson | | ✓ | | | | | |
| Dresser (stage) | | ✓ | | | | | |
| Dressmaker | | ✓ | ✓ | | | | |
| Driver | | | ✓ | | | | |
| Drug and alcohol counsellor | | | | | | | ✓ |
| Drycleaner | | | | | | ✓ | |
| Ecologist | | | | ✓ | | | |
| Economist | | | | | ✓ | | |
| Editor | ✓ | | | | | | |
| Editor (newspapers) | ✓ | | | | ✓ | | |
| Editorial cartoonist | | ✓ | | | | | |
| Educational psychologist | | | | ✓ | | | ✓ |

| | W | A | P | E | O | B | S |
|---|---|---|---|---|---|---|---|
| Electrical engineer | | | ✓ | ✓ | | | |
| Electrician | | | ✓ | | | | |
| Electronics engineer | | | ✓ | ✓ | | | |
| Elementary school teacher | | | | | | | ✓ |
| Embalmer | | ✓ | | | | | |
| Employment officer | | | | | ✓ | | ✓ |
| Engineering pattern maker | | ✓ | ✓ | | | | |
| Engineering technician | | | ✓ | | | | |
| English language teacher | ✓ | | | | | | ✓ |
| Engraver | | ✓ | | | | | |
| Entertainments officer | | ✓ | | ✓ | | | |
| Environmental health officer | | | ✓ | ✓ | | | |
| Equestrian | | | ✓ | | | | |
| Ergonomist | | | ✓ | ✓ | | | |
| Estate agent | | | | | ✓ | ✓ | |
| Estate manager | | | ✓ | ✓ | ✓ | | |
| Exhibition organizer | | ✓ | | | ✓ | | |
| Explosives expert | | | ✓ | ✓ | | | |
| | | | | | | | |
| Farmer | | | ✓ | | ✓ | | |
| Farm manager | | | ✓ | | ✓ | | |
| Farm worker | | | ✓ | | | | |
| Fashion buyer | | ✓ | | | ✓ | | |
| Fashion designer | | ✓ | | | | | |
| Film projectionist | | ✓ | | | | | |
| Film reviewer | ✓ | ✓ | | | | | |
| Financial analyst | | | | | ✓ | | |
| Financial controller | | | | | ✓ | ✓ | |
| Firefighter | | | ✓ | | | | |
| Fisheries officer | | | ✓ | | | | |
| Fisherman | | | ✓ | | | | |
| Fitter | | | ✓ | | | | |
| Flight attendant | | | | | | | ✓ |
| Florist | | ✓ | | | | | |
| Flyperson (theatre) | | | ✓ | | | | |
| Food hygiene inspector | | | | ✓ | | | |
| Food service worker | | | ✓ | | | | |
| Foreign correspondent | ✓ | | | | | | |

## Test Yourself!

| | W | A | P | E | O | B | S |
|---|---|---|---|---|---|---|---|
| Foreign language teacher | ✓ | | | | | | ✓ |
| Forensic pathologist | | | | ✓ | | | |
| Forensic psychologist | | | | ✓ | | | |
| Forensic scientist | | | | ✓ | | | |
| Forester | | | ✓ | | | | |
| Freelance writer | ✓ | | | | | | |
| Fund raiser | | | | | ✓ | ✓ | |
| Funeral director | | | | ✓ | | ✓ | |
| Furniture maker | | ✓ | ✓ | | | | |
| Gamekeeper | | | ✓ | | | | |
| Gardener | | ✓ | ✓ | | | | |
| Genealogist | | | | ✓ | | | |
| Geneticist | | | | ✓ | | | |
| Geochemist | | | | ✓ | | | |
| Geologist | | | | ✓ | | | |
| Glassblower | | ✓ | | | | | |
| Glazier | | ✓ | ✓ | | | | |
| Golf professional | | | ✓ | | ✓ | | |
| Graphic designer | | ✓ | | | | | |
| Grocer | | | | | ✓ | | |
| Groundsperson | | | ✓ | | | | |
| Guard | | | ✓ | | | | |
| Gunsmith | | ✓ | ✓ | | | | |
| Hairdresser | | ✓ | | | | | ✓ |
| Head teacher | | | | | ✓ | | ✓ |
| Health services administrator | | | | | ✓ | | |
| Health visitor | | | | | | | ✓ |
| Heating engineer | | | ✓ | | | | |
| Historian | ✓ | | | ✓ | | | |
| Homeopath | | | | ✓ | | | |
| Horologist | | | | ✓ | | | |
| Horticulturalist | | | ✓ | ✓ | | | |
| Hospital physicist | | | | ✓ | | | |
| Hospital porter | | | ✓ | | | | |

| | W | A | P | E | O | B | S |
|---|---|---|---|---|---|---|---|
| Hostel warden | | | | | | | ✔ |
| Hotel manager | | | | | ✔ | ✔ | |
| House parent | | | | | | | ✔ |
| Housing manager | | | ✔ | | | | ✔ |
| Human resources manager | | | | | ✔ | ✔ | ✔ |
| Hydrographic surveyor | | | | ✔ | | | |
| Hydrologist | | | | ✔ | | | |
| | | | | | | | |
| Illustrator | | ✔ | | | | | |
| Immunologist | | | | ✔ | | | |
| Importer/exporter | | | | | ✔ | ✔ | |
| Industrial designer | | ✔ | | | | | |
| Industrial nurse | | | | ✔ | | | ✔ |
| Industrial relations officer | | | | | | ✔ | ✔ |
| Information officer | ✔ | | | | | | |
| Information scientist | ✔ | | | ✔ | | | |
| Instrument and control engineer | | | ✔ | ✔ | | | |
| Instrument maker | | | ✔ | ✔ | | | |
| Insurance adjuster | | | | ✔ | | | |
| Insurange agent | | | | ✔ | | | |
| Interior designer | | ✔ | | | | | |
| Interpreter | ✔ | | | | | | |
| Interviewer | ✔ | | | | | | ✔ |
| | | | | | | | |
| Jewellery maker | | ✔ | | | | | |
| Jockey | | | ✔ | | | | |
| Joiner | | ✔ | ✔ | | | | |
| Journalist | ✔ | | | | | | |
| Judge | ✔ | | | | | | |
| Justices clerk | ✔ | | | ✔ | | | |
| | | | | | | | |
| Laboratory technician | | | | ✔ | | | |
| Landscape architect | | ✔ | | | | | |
| Language teacher | ✔ | | | | | | ✔ |
| Lawyer | ✔ | | | | | | |
| Legal executive | ✔ | | | | | | |

## Test Yourself!

| | W | A | P | E | O | B | S |
|---|---|---|---|---|---|---|---|
| Leisure centre staff | | ✔ | ✔ | | ✔ | | |
| Liberal studies teacher | ✔ | | | | | | ✔ |
| Librarian | ✔ | | | ✔ | ✔ | | |
| Library assistant | ✔ | | | ✔ | | | |
| Lighthouse keeper | | | ✔ | | | | |
| Lighting technician | | ✔ | ✔ | | | | |
| Linguist | ✔ | | | | | | |
| Literary agent | ✔ | | | | | ✔ | |
| Literary critic | ✔ | | | | | | |
| Lock keeper | | | ✔ | | | | |
| Locksmith | | | ✔ | | | | |
| Locomotive engineer | | | ✔ | ✔ | | | |
| Lorry driver | | | ✔ | | | | |
| Machinist | ✔ | ✔ | | | | | |
| Maintenance technician | | | ✔ | | | | |
| Maître d' | | ✔ | | | | | |
| Make-up artist | | ✔ | | | | | |
| Management consultant | | | | | ✔ | | |
| Managing director | | | | | ✔ | | |
| Marine biologist | | | | ✔ | | | |
| Market gardner | ✔ | ✔ | | | ✔ | | |
| Marketing manager | ✔ | | | | ✔ | | |
| Market researcher | | | ✔ | ✔ | | | |
| Masseur/masseuse | ✔ | | | | | | ✔ |
| Materials scientist | | | | ✔ | | | |
| Mathematician | | | | ✔ | | | |
| Mechanic | | | ✔ | | | | |
| Mechanical engineer | | | ✔ | ✔ | | | |
| Medical illustrator | ✔ | | ✔ | | | | |
| Medical records officer | | | | ✔ | | | |
| Medical representative | | | | ✔ | ✔ | | |
| Medical secretary | | | | ✔ | | | ✔ |
| Mental nurse | | | | ✔ | | | ✔ |
| Merchandiser | ✔ | | ✔ | | | | |
| Merchant seaman | | ✔ | | | | | |
| Metallurgist | | | | ✔ | | | |

|                              | W | A | P | E | O | B | S |
|------------------------------|---|---|---|---|---|---|---|
| Meteorologist                |   |   |   | ✔ |   |   |   |
| Microbiologist               |   |   |   | ✔ |   |   |   |
| Midwife                      |   |   |   | ✔ |   |   | ✔ |
| Milkman                      |   |   | ✔ |   |   |   |   |
| Miller                       | ✔ |   | ✔ |   |   |   |   |
| Milliner                     | ✔ |   |   |   |   |   |   |
| Miner                        |   |   | ✔ |   |   |   |   |
| Minister of religion         |   |   |   |   |   |   | ✔ |
| Model (fashion)              | ✔ |   |   |   |   |   |   |
| Model maker                  | ✔ |   | ✔ |   |   |   |   |
| Museum assistant             | ✔ |   |   | ✔ |   |   |   |
| Musician                     | ✔ |   |   |   |   |   |   |
| Music producer               | ✔ |   |   |   |   | ✔ |   |
| Music therapist              | ✔ |   |   |   |   |   | ✔ |
|                              |   |   |   |   |   |   |   |
| Nanny                        |   |   |   |   |   |   | ✔ |
| Nature conservancy warden    |   |   | ✔ | ✔ |   |   |   |
| Navigating officer           |   |   | ✔ | ✔ |   |   |   |
| Negotiator                   |   |   |   |   | ✔ |   |   |
| Neurosurgeon                 |   |   |   | ✔ |   |   |   |
| Notary public                |   | ✔ |   |   |   |   |   |
| Novelist                     |   | ✔ |   |   |   |   |   |
| Nuclear physicist            |   |   |   | ✔ |   |   |   |
| Nurse                        |   |   |   | ✔ |   |   | ✔ |
| Nursery nurse                |   |   |   |   |   |   | ✔ |
| Nutritionist                 |   |   |   | ✔ |   |   |   |
|                              |   |   |   |   |   |   |   |
| Obstetrician                 |   |   |   | ✔ |   |   | ✔ |
| Occupational psychologist    |   |   |   | ✔ |   | ✔ | ✔ |
| Occupational therapist       |   | ✔ | ✔ |   |   |   | ✔ |
| Office cleaner               |   |   | ✔ |   |   |   |   |
| Office machinery mechanic    |   |   | ✔ |   |   |   |   |
| Office manager               |   |   |   |   | ✔ | ✔ |   |
| Oil rig worker               |   |   | ✔ |   |   |   |   |
| Operational researcher       |   |   |   | ✔ |   |   |   |
| Ophthalmic optician          |   |   |   | ✔ |   |   |   |
| Optician (dispensing)        |   |   |   | ✔ |   | ✔ |   |

# Test Yourself!

|  | W | A | P | E | O | B | S |
|---|---|---|---|---|---|---|---|
| Organization and methods officer |  |  |  | ✔ | ✔ |  |  |
| Orthodontist |  |  |  | ✔ |  |  | ✔ |
| Orthoptist |  |  |  | ✔ |  |  |  |
| Osteopath |  |  | ✔ | ✔ |  |  | ✔ |
| Outplacement consultant |  |  |  |  | ✔ | ✔ |  |
| Panel beater |  |  | ✔ |  |  |  |  |
| Paramedic |  |  |  | ✔ |  |  | ✔ |
| Patent agent | ✔ |  |  |  |  | ✔ |  |
| Patent examiner | ✔ |  |  | ✔ |  |  |  |
| Pathologist |  |  |  | ✔ |  |  |  |
| Pattern cutter |  | ✔ | ✔ |  |  |  |  |
| Personal trainer |  |  |  |  |  |  | ✔ |
| Pharmacist |  |  |  | ✔ |  | ✔ |  |
| Pharmacologist |  |  |  | ✔ |  |  |  |
| Philosopher | ✔ |  |  |  |  |  |  |
| Photographer |  | ✔ |  |  |  |  |  |
| Photographic technician |  | ✔ | ✔ |  |  |  |  |
| Physical education teacher |  |  | ✔ |  |  |  | ✔ |
| Physicist |  |  |  | ✔ |  |  | ✔ |
| Physiotherapist |  | ✔ |  | ✔ |  |  | ✔ |
| Piano teacher |  | ✔ |  |  |  |  | ✔ |
| Piano tuner |  | ✔ |  |  |  |  |  |
| Picture framer |  | ✔ |  |  |  |  |  |
| Pilot (airplane) |  |  | ✔ | ✔ |  |  |  |
| Pilot (coastal) |  |  | ✔ |  |  |  |  |
| Plasterer |  | ✔ | ✔ |  |  |  |  |
| Play leader |  |  |  |  |  |  | ✔ |
| Plumber |  |  | ✔ |  |  |  |  |
| Poet | ✔ |  |  |  |  |  |  |
| Police dog handler |  |  | ✔ |  |  |  |  |
| Police officer |  |  | ✔ |  |  |  | ✔ |
| Political agent | ✔ |  |  |  | ✔ |  |  |
| Politician |  |  |  |  | ✔ |  | ✔ |
| Pool and spa operator |  |  | ✔ |  |  |  |  |
| Poster designer |  | ✔ |  |  |  |  |  |

| | W | A | P | E | O | B | S |
|---|---|---|---|---|---|---|---|
| Postman/woman | | | ✔ | | | | |
| Post office clerk | | | | ✔ | | | |
| Potter | | ✔ | | | | | |
| Press agent | ✔ | | | | | | |
| Principal nursing officer | | | | ✔ | | | ✔ |
| Printer | | ✔ | ✔ | | | | |
| Prison officer | | | ✔ | | | | ✔ |
| Probation officer | | | | | | | ✔ |
| Producer (films) | | ✔ | | | ✔ | ✔ | |
| Production manager | | ✔ | ✔ | | | | |
| Programmer | | | | ✔ | ✔ | | |
| Property negotiator | | | | | | ✔ | |
| Prosthetics engineer | | ✔ | ✔ | | | | |
| Psychiatric social worker | | | | | | | ✔ |
| Psychiatrist | ✔ | | | ✔ | | | ✔ |
| Psychoanalyst | ✔ | | | | | | ✔ |
| Psychologist | | | | ✔ | | | ✔ |
| Psychotherapist | ✔ | ✔ | | | | | ✔ |
| Publican | | | ✔ | | | | |
| Publicity agent | ✔ | ✔ | | | | ✔ | |
| Public relations executive | ✔ | ✔ | | | | ✔ | |
| Publisher | ✔ | | | | | ✔ | |
| Purchasing manager | | | | | ✔ | ✔ | |
| Purser | | | | | ✔ | | |
| Quality controller | | | ✔ | ✔ | | | |
| Quality inspector | | | ✔ | | | | |
| Quantity surveyor | | | ✔ | | ✔ | | |
| Racing car driver | | | ✔ | | | | |
| Radiographer | | | | ✔ | | | |
| Railway guard | | | ✔ | | | | |
| Rating valuation officer | | | | | ✔ | | |
| Receptionist | ✔ | ✔ | | | | | ✔ |
| Recording engineer | | | | ✔ | | | |
| Reflexologist | | ✔ | | ✔ | | | ✔ |
| Remedial teacher | | | | | | | ✔ |

**Test Yourself!**

| | W | A | P | E | O | B | S |
|---|---|---|---|---|---|---|---|
| Renovator | | ✔ | ✔ | | | | |
| Reporter | ✔ | | | | | | |
| Restorer | | ✔ | ✔ | | | | |
| Retail assistant | | | | | | ✔ | |
| Retail manager | | | | | ✔ | ✔ | |
| Roofer | | | ✔ | | | | |
| | | | | | | | |
| Saddler | | ✔ | ✔ | | | | |
| Sailor | | | ✔ | | | | |
| Sales executive | | | | | | ✔ | |
| Sales manager | | | | | | ✔ | |
| Salesperson | | | | | | ✔ | |
| Sales trainer | | | | | | ✔ | ✔ |
| Science teacher | | | | ✔ | | | ✔ |
| Science writer | ✔ | | | ✔ | | | |
| Scientific instrument maker | | ✔ | ✔ | | | | |
| Scriptwriter | ✔ | | | | | | |
| Sculptor | | ✔ | | | | | |
| Secretary/PA | ✔ | ✔ | | | | | |
| Securities analyst | | | | ✔ | ✔ | | |
| Security officer | | | ✔ | | | | |
| Session musician | | ✔ | | | | | |
| Set designer | | ✔ | | | | | |
| Shepherd | | | ✔ | | | | |
| Shipping and forwarding officer | | | | | ✔ | | |
| Shop fitter | | ✔ | ✔ | | | | |
| Sign writer | | ✔ | | | | | |
| Silversmith | | ✔ | | | | | |
| Social scientist | ✔ | | | ✔ | | | ✔ |
| Social worker | | | | | | | ✔ |
| Soldier | | | ✔ | | | | |
| Solicitor | ✔ | | | | | | |
| Sound engineer | | ✔ | ✔ | | | | |
| Space salesperson | | | | | | ✔ | |
| Speech therapist | | | | | | | ✔ |
| Sports coach | | | ✔ | | | | ✔ |

| | W | A | P | E | O | B | S |
|---|---|---|---|---|---|---|---|
| Sports official (referee) | | | ✔ | | | | |
| Stagehand | | ✔ | | | | | |
| Stage manager | | ✔ | | | | ✔ | |
| Statistician | | | | ✔ | ✔ | | |
| Stockbroker | | | | | ✔ | ✔ | |
| Stock controller | | | | | ✔ | | |
| Stone mason | | ✔ | | | | | |
| Studio assistant | | ✔ | | | | | |
| Stunt performer | | | ✔ | | | | |
| Surgeon | | | | ✔ | | | |
| Surveyor | | | | ✔ | ✔ | | |
| Systems analyst | | | | ✔ | ✔ | | |
| | | | | | | | |
| Tailor | | ✔ | | | | | |
| Taxidermist | | ✔ | | | | | |
| Taxi driver | | | ✔ | | | | |
| Tax inspector | | | | | ✔ | | |
| Teacher | | | | | | | ✔ |
| Teacher of art/craft | | ✔ | | | | | ✔ |
| Teacher of handicapped | | | | | | | ✔ |
| Technical illustrator | | ✔ | | ✔ | | | |
| Technical representative | | | ✔ | ✔ | | ✔ | |
| Technical writer | | ✔ | | ✔ | | | |
| Telecommunications engineer | | | | ✔ | ✔ | | |
| Telephonist | ✔ | | | | | | ✔ |
| Television engineer | | | | ✔ | ✔ | | |
| Television production assistant | | ✔ | | | | | |
| Thatcher | | | ✔ | | | | |
| Theatre administrator | | ✔ | | | ✔ | | |
| Tiler | | | ✔ | | | | |
| Tool maker | | | ✔ | | | | |
| Toy maker | | ✔ | | | | | |
| Tracer | | ✔ | | | | | |
| Traffic warden | | | ✔ | | | | |
| Train driver | | | ✔ | | | | |

**Test Yourself!**

|                          | W | A | P | E | O | B | S |
|--------------------------|---|---|---|---|---|---|---|
| Training officer         | ✔ |   | ✔ |   |   |   | ✔ |
| Translator               | ✔ |   |   |   |   |   |   |
| Transport manager        |   |   | ✔ |   | ✔ |   |   |
| Travel agent             |   | ✔ |   | ✔ |   |   |   |
| Truck driver             |   |   | ✔ |   |   |   |   |
| Turf accountant          |   |   |   | ✔ |   |   |   |
| Umpire                   |   |   | ✔ |   |   |   | ✔ |
| Underwriter              |   |   |   | ✔ |   |   |   |
| Union negotiator         |   |   |   |   |   | ✔ |   |
| Upholsterer              |   | ✔ |   |   |   |   |   |
| Urban planner            |   | ✔ |   | ✔ |   |   |   |
| Veterinary nurse         |   |   | ✔ |   |   |   |   |
| Veterinary surgeon       |   |   | ✔ | ✔ |   |   |   |
| Vision mixer             |   | ✔ |   | ✔ |   |   |   |
| Vocational counsellor    |   |   |   |   |   |   | ✔ |
| Waiter/waitress          |   | ✔ |   |   |   |   | ✔ |
| Watch repairer           |   |   | ✔ |   |   |   |   |
| Welder                   |   |   | ✔ |   |   |   |   |
| Window dresser           |   | ✔ |   |   |   |   |   |
| Word processor operator  | ✔ |   |   |   |   |   |   |
| Work study officer       |   |   | ✔ |   | ✔ |   |   |
| Writer                   | ✔ |   |   |   |   |   |   |
| Youth worker             |   |   |   |   |   |   | ✔ |
| Zoo keeper               |   | ✔ |   | ✔ |   |   |   |
| Zoologist                |   |   |   | ✔ |   |   |   |